Trauma and the 12 Ste,
The Workbook

"With great respect for the twelve steps, Marich and Dansiger challenge the greatest barrier to many who struggle to attain recovery—their trauma. Unhealed trauma is the most significant factor in the development of an addiction, and it is a significant relapse trigger. To be able to genuinely embrace twelve-step work, a person struggling needs to feel safe in their own bodies, and they need a regulated nervous system and a calm limbic system. By incorporating trauma-responsive exercises, meditation, and expressive arts into twelve-step work, readers will be able to utilize the gifts of the steps. This workbook offers a foundation to recovery that many only find years after possibly staying sober but not finding joy in recovery. Jamie and Stephen are on my gratitude list!"

—CLAUDIA BLACK PH.D., addiction specialist and author of *It Will Never Happen to Me*

"An essential companion to Dr. Marich's excellent *Trauma and the 12 Steps,* this workbook provides a unique trauma-focused approach to working the twelve steps that makes them more accessible and includes step-specific meditations and expressive arts exercises. This volume will be invaluable for anyone on the path of recovery for whom trauma is co-occurring—whether they are new to twelve-step recovery or a veteran of the process."

—DAN MAGER, MSW, author of *Some Assembly Required*

"This workbook is not a buzzword foray into the recovery/industrial/publishing complex. Based on their personal recoveries and clinical experience, Marich and Dansiger provide a fresh and compassionate guide through the twelve steps as seen through the lens of trauma. The authors have captured the dynamic essence of the steps, freed from the *Big Book*'s 1930s uninformed societal language and perceived patriarchy. Gentle suggestions on how to approach the more challenging aspects of the steps—such as God or Higher Power—removes some obstacles that have led some to throw the baby out with the bathwater. This is a sincere and informed offering to help achieve the goals of the steps that seemed out of reach for those dealing with trauma to become happily and usefully whole."

—JAY DEE DAUGHERTY, New York State Certified Addiction Recovery Coach and drummer in the Patti Smith Group

"Twelve-step recovery saved my life, and then EMDR therapy and other trauma work saved my life once again. For decades these have been seen as separate, but now people in the recovery community and in the addiction field are seeing more clearly that trauma and addiction are deeply linked. Marich and Dansiger have acknowledged, studied, written, taught and acted upon this knowledge extensively, and in *Trauma and the 12 Steps—The Workbook*, they add a tool that can save a lot of twelve-step members much pain and suffering in early recovery and beyond. Anyone in recovery could start their journey here or take another trip through the steps. I am adding this workbook to my own personal resource list and for those I work with as an addiction professional. Much gratitude to Jamie and Steve for this offering!"

—MACKENZIE PHILLIPS, recovery advocate, actress, and *New York Times* bestselling author of *High on Arrival*

"I was already twelve years into my recovery when someone mentioned that "trauma" could apply to me. I had a visceral response and fought it with almost the same amount of energy that I immersed myself into it. In the ensuing years, as a devoted twelve-stepper, I have tried to marry the wisdom and beauty of the twelve steps with the healing of trauma work. Now, in 2023, in meetings I hear people talking about trauma a lot more. There is an (r)evolutionary conversation happening in recovery that is so necessary for the twelve-step community and our healing. Workbooks like this will be an essential tool to help us integrate synergistically these two perspectives. I deeply respect Jamie and Steve for their work and for their leadership and giving this gift of profound healing to all of those still suffering."

—DAN GRIFFIN, author *A Man's Way through the Twelve Steps*

"I wish I had this workbook when I got sober. With gratitude and a deep breath, I highly endorse *Trauma and the 12-Steps—The Workbook* as a bridge between what we know works in twelve-step recovery and what we need to incorporate from our current trauma-informed knowledge base. This workbook will guide the reader towards an experiential relationship with each step. All too often, step work has become a strictly cognitive exercise, leading people in recovery to a perpetual whack-a-mole game with their ongoing, unresolved symptoms. Jamie and Stephen have combined their decades-long personal experiences in recovery with their expertise as trauma therapists to bring the steps alive in a comprehensive and holistic way, and I applaud them for it."

—INGRID CLAYTON, PhD, author of *Believing Me*

TRAUMA AND THE 12 STEPS
THE WORKBOOK

TRAUMA
12
AND THE
STEPS
THE _WORKBOOK_

Exercises and Meditations
for Addiction, Trauma Recovery,
and Working the 12 Steps

JAMIE MARICH, PHD, AND STEPHEN DANSIGER, PSYD, MFT

North Atlantic Books
Huichin, unceded Ohlone land
Berkeley, California

Published by   Cover art © dzubanovska via Getty Images
North Atlantic Books   Cover design by Jasmine Hromjak
Huichin, unceded Ohlone land   Book design by Happenstance Type-O-Rama
Berkeley, California

Printed in the United States of America

Trauma and the 12 Steps—The Workbook: Exercises and Meditations for Addiction, Trauma Recovery, and Working the 12 Steps is sponsored and published by North Atlantic Books, an educational nonprofit based in the unceded Ohlone land Huichin (Berkeley, CA) that collaborates with partners to develop cross-cultural perspectives; nurture holistic views of art, science, the humanities, and healing; and seed personal and global transformation by publishing work on the relationship of body, spirit, and nature.

North Atlantic Books' publications are distributed to the US trade and internationally by Penguin Random House Publisher Services. For further information, visit our website at www.northatlanticbooks.com.

Library of Congress Cataloging-in-Publication Data

Names: Marich, Jamie, author. | Dansiger, Stephen, author.
Title: Trauma and the 12 steps–the workbook : exercises and meditations
    for addiction, trauma recovery, and working the 12 steps / Jamie Marich
    and Stephen Dansiger.
Description: Berkeley, California : North Atlantic Books, [2023]
Identifiers: LCCN 2022057386 (print) | LCCN 2022057387 (ebook) | ISBN
    9781623179328 (trade paperback) | ISBN 9781623179335 (ebook)
Subjects: LCSH: Twelve-step programs. | Psychic trauma–Treatment. |
    Post-traumatic stress disorder–Treatment. | Substance abuse–Treatment.
Classification: LCC RC564 .M2953 2023 (print) | LCC RC564 (ebook) | DDC
    616.86/06–dc23/eng/20230414
LC record available at https://lccn.loc.gov/2022057386
LC ebook record available at https://lccn.loc.gov/2022057387

1 2 3 4 5 6 7 8 9 VERSA 27 26 25 24 23

North Atlantic Books is committed to the protection of our environment. We print on recycled paper whenever possible and partner with printers who strive to use environmentally responsible practices.

A Note about Language Modification

Comprehending the language of recovery can be a difficult task for any newcomer, especially one who has experienced language as a means of wounding.

—JAMIE MARICH, *TRAUMA AND THE 12 STEPS: AN INCLUSIVE GUIDE TO ENHANCING RECOVERY*

The key to making anything more trauma-informed is to modify language or concepts so that they fit better with your life experiences and understanding. In our experience, many trauma survivors struggle to benefit from the twelve steps when they are introduced in a manner that is rigid and inflexible. We give specific examples many times throughout this workbook on how you can modify language. You have complete permission to modify language, especially around spiritual concepts or words that the authors of the twelve steps originally wrote to be very gendered. We encourage such modifications, so do not feel that you are working any less of a twelve-step program in needing to make them.

Contents

To Anna David, in gratitude!
Thank you for planting the seeds in our mind
that blossomed into this offering.

Foreword

Let me say upfront that the twelve steps have transformed my life.

Though I hadn't known it, I had long been seeking rules for living and so when I walked into one of my first twelve-step meetings and saw a list of the twelve steps on the wall, I thought, "Well, nothing could be worse than the steps I've been following, so I may as well give these a try."

I had no idea what any of the words in the twelve steps really meant, and the fact that some of them included the word *God* definitely freaked me out, but I was willing.

Turns out that willingness was all it took.

Roughly a decade and a half into sobriety, as I continued to work the twelve steps, I realized it was time to face the trauma I'd long since avoided. I had actually known I was destined for trauma therapy since I'd first heard of its existence but the idea of paying money to cry my eyes out didn't appeal. I waited, in fact, until I was going through a breakup that already left me crying my eyes out to finally give it a try. I figured if I was going to be crying all the time, I might as well have a quiet place to do it, and possibly get this trauma thing worked out at the same time.

Luckily, I know some of the world's greatest EMDR experts and so I reached out to Steve Dansiger. He referred me to a therapist who, over multiple sessions, guided me through EMDR. It was as foreign to me as the twelve steps had been when I first spied them on the wall, but I was desperate to feel better, which meant I was willing. Again.

Processing my trauma has been as profound and transformative as the twelve steps. It allowed me to break through thought patterns I'd assumed were too emotionally carved into my brain to ever shift, and I truly feel like I began to see myself for the first time.

Once I discovered the significance of trauma work, I asked Jamie—the other great EMDR expert I knew—why she and Steve had never created a twelve-step guide for trauma. They were as familiar with the twelve steps as they were with trauma so if anyone was going to do it, shouldn't it be them?

Luckily for all of us, this became their next project, and they've done it exquisitely. Their deep understanding of not just the importance of their mission but also the sacredness of it imbues this workbook with the kind of depth and weight that's required. By combining their shared expertise—which includes the twelve steps, meditation, and even expressive arts work—they've created something magical that no one else on earth could.

Going through this book isn't the same thing as attending a twelve-step meeting, working with a sponsor, or going to see a trauma therapist, but it's as close as you're going to get. It will bring you closer to seeing what others around you surely already do: you're glorious. And the book you're holding can help you to feel it.

—ANNA DAVID, JOURNALIST, BEST-SELLING AUTHOR
OF *PARTY GIRL,* AND FOUNDER OF LEGACY LAUNCH
PAD PUBLISHING

Preface to the Revised and Expanded Edition (2023)

I describe myself as both the biggest fan and the biggest critic of twelve-step recovery. Thankfully my recovery teaches me that two things can be true at the same time!

My first sponsor Janet Leff (1941–2017) taught me about twelve-step recovery in 2001 when I worked as a language assistant and humanitarian aid worker in postwar Bosnia and Herzegovina. My family is of mixed Slavic ancestry, primarily Croatian, and I felt a pull to the land affected by the brutal war that ravaged the countries of the former Yugoslavia from 1991–1995. Having just finished my undergraduate degree and feeling rather aimless in life due to my own struggles with untreated mental illness and addiction, something inside of me suggested that I would find answers by spending time in my literal homeland. Janet, an American social worker, relocated to Bosnia and Herzegovina in her retirement to help with the emergence of some fledging treatment programs and other initiatives. She correctly identified that addiction was an issue for me and used the philosophies of twelve-step recovery to begin validating my addiction as something that was not my fault while also giving me the tools of the steps to help me bring about meaningful lifestyle change. Janet was also the first person to give me the language of trauma to frame so many of my struggles with mental illness. Up until that point I believed that trauma was something that only veterans or people who survived war experienced. And interestingly, there I was working with so many young survivors of a recent, literal war and I began to see common threads in our respective struggles. Janet famously said to me, "Maybe the warzone you survived was your house."

I tell the complete version of this story in my book *Trauma and the 12 Steps: An Inclusive Guide to Enhancing Recovery,* which is arguably the book I am best known for in my career as a therapist, writer, and trauma educator. Originally published in 2012 and then released by North Atlantic Books in a revised and expanded form in 2020, my work in this area seeks to show how the twelve steps originally developed in the 1930s can still be useful for people struggling with addictions, compulsions, and related issues. The work also acknowledges that the steps can use some language modifications. Moreover, cultures surrounding twelve-step recovery are usually in need of a serious update to account for the realities of unhealed trauma and its impact on the human experience. These cultures include, but are not limited to, twelve-step meetings in the community and treatment centers or other programs that operate with a serious commitment to uphold twelve-step and disease model paradigms of addiction.

I've grown so frustrated with the disregard for trauma that I see in both meetings in the community and professional treatment settings, I sometimes surprise myself that I've not just walked away from it all and dismissed the twelve steps as outdated. Indeed, many of my contemporaries in the helping professions have long disregarded twelve-step recovery as archaic and even dangerous. Yes, I call out the dangerous elements in *Trauma and the 12 Steps* (e.g., abusive sponsorship dynamics, problematic slogans, abrasive rigidity to working a program, and taking advantage of new members to any given twelve-step program—especially sexually). Yet for me and others like me (including my coauthor on this workbook project, Dr. Stephen Dansiger), there is still healing power in the steps themselves. A few language updates may be required to make them more trauma-informed and user-friendly, and such modifications are what my advocacy seeks to promote.

There is a concept in religious trauma recovery that is growing in recognition: Deconstruction and Reconstruction. The journey I've been on with trauma-informing the twelve steps for over a decade now can be described as such. I've picked it all apart, especially when I realized just how harmful certain aspects of twelve-step recovery can be when placed in the hands of counselors, sponsors, and members of various fellowships who haven't yet come to terms with the impact of trauma on their own lives. By engaging in this necessary criticism, I've managed to salvage the components that still work for me and seemingly for countless others. And embracing these gifts also emboldens me to highlight where the problems exist and call for new, more inclusive recovery paradigms. I am delighted that so many people have found benefit in the original *Trauma and the 12 Steps* and its related projects over the years. I hope that this expanded workbook will add to the growing collection of resources as we seek to address the interplay of trauma and addiction.

A friend in long-term recovery recently asked me what my recovery is looking like these days in terms of what I do to *work a program* or keep myself healthy and well after twenty years. As I shared with him, I do not go to twelve-step meetings very regularly anymore even though I am absolutely clear that abstinence and refraining from alcohol and controlled substances continue to serve me best. I remain in close contact with my long-term sponsor Dharl (whom I also write about more fully in *Trauma and the 12 Steps*) and a close-knit group of other folks in recovery who feel like my family of choice. There are many queer folks and several other "Rebel Twelve-Steppers" in this group of loving people surrounding me. Presently I find more nourishment from yoga and meditation groups that meet with an aim of recovery more than I benefit from traditional meetings, and I also remain actively engaged with my personal trauma therapist. Even though meetings are not such a critical part of my life anymore, the steps and ideas of twelve-step recovery are. They accompany me in every other piece of work that I do in my life, both personally and professionally. I realize that the steps and the path of total abstinence may not be a fit for everyone, yet my hope is that they can continue to be shared with people who are suffering in as compassionate and trauma-responsive a way as possible.

—JAMIE MARICH (AKRON, OHIO)

✳ ✳ ✳

Over the last couple of years (2020–2022), like many people I have met along the way, I have had some of my old traumas resurface.

These traumas can manifest in many ways. For some people I talked to, they manifested as a reengagement with substances, or an outbreak of behaviors that had been dormant. For others, it was problems with sadness, grief, depression, or anxiety. In my case, at over thirty years of recovery, it resulted in my seeking yet another trip through the twelve steps, in addition to anything and everything else I do to stay healthy. In my both/and approach to my recovery, all hands were on deck and all new and well-worn ideas were welcome.

Back in 2012 when I came upon Jamie's work on *Trauma and the 12 Steps,* I knew a number of things. One was that this was one of my people. Another was that the twelve steps need not be static or stagnant, but can be alive and dynamic. And the most important thing was that if we honored the role of trauma and trauma healing in recovery, we could continue to change the world.

My meeting Jamie was just one of many steps on my journey that has been blessed with great ideas and people throughout. I feel like my major guides in this process were all trauma-informed before anyone used that verbiage. I have always been treated with great compassion and loving kindness by sponsors, I have found friends on the path who did not judge each other for the bumpiness of our individual recovery voyages, and I have found twelve-step groups that intuitively worked in ways that honored trauma. I am well aware that this has not been the case for everyone. It is in the spirit of increasing access to a lifelong process, a community endeavor, and a sustainable healing path that we offer this new edition of our step workbook to you.

My years of substance addiction were a roller coaster. I discovered alcohol and cannabis as a twelve-year-old, which in hindsight I see was spurred on by trauma, both intergenerational and event-based. I became more and more involved with those two substances until the age of sixteen, when I added much more to the mix as I left for a much too early entry into college. All of this was side by side with a burgeoning career as a drummer in punk rock and art rock bands, creating an escalation of my commitment to heavy drinking and drug use.

My scheduled four-year college stint ended after two years in the university hospital, my music career stopped and started and sputtered and crawled, and at the age of twenty-six, my friend Maggie took me to my first AA meeting. Her implicit trauma-informed approach was a steadfast commitment to "attraction, not promotion" that allowed me to inspect the whole thing on my own but with her kind support and oversight always available. I then met friends new and old in the meetings ("I was wondering why Keith wasn't at the bar anymore and where he went . . .") and started doing what was suggested. I did service for groups, I spent a lot of time bopping around the Lower East Side of New York City to meetings, went to coffee shops in between, and started to feel the sunshine on my face. I went to an AA retreat at a Zen monastery, learned how to sit meditation, and began practicing mindfulness regularly (now at over thirty years and counting). I quit my music career, just as one band got signed to a major label, so I could stay focused on recovery.

When it was time to explore working again, I went to the Employment Program for Recovering Alcoholics (which still exists) and found myself suited to be a high school English teacher. My trauma education through direct experience continued when, after my first year of teaching, there was racial unrest in the school neighborhood. I taught about what we witnessed and experienced on the fly, was trained to teach about it in a more structured manner, and went on to facilitate conversations on systemic oppression and issues of diversity for almost fifteen years.

By the time I became a therapist in the early 2000s, I was steeped in the language of trauma and mindfulness. So, when I was introduced to EMDR therapy, it made a lot of sense very quickly and became my primary therapeutic modality. Before I met Jamie and discovered her book, I knew that the twelve steps were not antithetical to trauma recovery, and that trauma recovery was available through the twelve steps when the practitioners and sponsors had the right support and framework.

What is it like now? I actually go to a good number of meetings in more than one fellowship. I am doing a lot of online meetings for a number of reasons, not the least of which is the international flavor, and by default, more diverse populations. The twelve steps are an integral part of my multifaceted recovery plan. I seek help from a trauma therapist. I lead and participate in Buddhist meditation groups regularly, and also have found my way back to other forms of spirituality, including the religion of my birth, Judaism. I write and coauthor books on clinician self-care, mindfulness, anger management, EMDR therapy, and addiction.

All this is to say that I have an integrated and integrative life. My hope for you is that this book might help you on a twelve-step journey, whether you are brand new to it or multiple decades in, that will allow you the deep healing and increased presence that delivers a life worth living, fully alive, living authentically. A trauma-responsive twelve-step journey can be a powerful driver or one aspect of such a life. May you be free from fear, healthy, and happy. And, may you be at ease.

—STEPHEN DANSIGER (LOS ANGELES, CALIFORNIA)

Introduction

Relapse is prevalent in many behavioral disorders, especially addiction. Although various models can explain relapse, the common theme is that poor self-efficacy and high volumes of negative emotion, coupled with poor coping skills, put an individual at greatest risk for relapsing on alcohol or other drugs following a period of sobriety. In simpler terms, if you don't like yourself and you deal with mostly troubling emotions, you are going to have a hard time staying sober—especially if you haven't learned any meaningful, effective ways to cope and to manage emotions.

—JAMIE MARICH, *TRAUMA AND THE 12 STEPS: AN INCLUSIVE GUIDE TO ENHANCING RECOVERY*

In the various twelve-step programs, members emphasize the importance of working the steps *in order to cope, to manage emotions, and ultimately to recover.* What does that really mean . . . to *work* a step? How does one actually *work* a step? Like many answers people receive in twelve-step programs, it largely depends on whom you ask.

Some people are very by the book . . . literally. If you are a member of Alcoholics Anonymous (AA), a sponsor may guide you to work the steps directly as they are instructed in the "Big Book" of AA. First published in 1939 and now in its fourth edition (with a fifth coming soon), the Big Book is very specific about how you can work some steps and very vague about others. If you are a member of Narcotics Anonymous, it's likely that you've been instructed to use a step workbook published by that fellowship. With hundreds of fellowships growing from the original seeds planted by AA, lots of books now exist and there are a great many ideas on the market and in the public forum on how to work the steps.

Many twelve-step sponsors guide their sponsees through the steps in the exact same way that their sponsors showed them. Passing on your own experience, strength, and hope as a sponsor can be a beautiful thing. Yet, if it's relayed with the rigidity of "if this way worked for me, it will work for you," problems can ensue. As explained in *Trauma and the 12 Steps: An Inclusive Guide to Enhancing Recovery* (the book on which this workbook is based), this inflexible mentality is what can make working the twelve steps a retraumatizing trap for people struggling in recovery. Jamie writes, "The best way to look at flexibility in a trauma-sensitive context is that it represents the ability to meet newcomers where they are *at* in the recovery or change process. Flexibility is the opposite of rigidity, and rigidity is a trait on display at so many recovery meetings and in many treatment centers."*

We are happy to present you with this trauma-responsive step work guide as a companion piece to *Trauma and the 12 Steps* or to be used on its own. Since the publication of the original *Trauma and the Twelve Steps: A Complete Guide to Enhancing Recovery* in 2012, Jamie has received multiple requests for a step guide that takes trauma into consideration. As she worked on the new edition of *Trauma and the 12 Steps: An Inclusive Guide to Enhancing Recovery*, she responded to the challenge and brought her longtime collaborator Dr. Stephen (Steve) Dansiger on board to create this new resource.

As Steve reflects, "I can't deal with charts, graphs, and columns; I just had to turn them onto their side and make a narrative." He explains that people in programs have different philosophies. In his early recovery, he had two sponsors and experienced directly the peril of mixed messages. His first sponsor would tell him to waltz Steps One, Two, and Three over and over again the first year, and then wanted him to exit this waltz pattern and dive into the mosh pit of Step Four. His other sponsor from those first years suggested he dive into all the steps in order as soon as possible in the first year. When all was said and done, Steve found a way to combine those two approaches and make them his own. However, many other people might despair on hearing conflicting philosophies from different folks around the rooms of recovery and may even leave the program in frustration as a result. Our feeling is that there is no one right way to work any of the steps, as long as you are working them.

In this workbook, we guide you through the twelve steps, breaking down each one in a trauma-focused way. A meditation or coping skill of focus is included for each respective step. Traditional writing and expressive arts exercises are given for each step to help people on various stages of their recovery journey work the steps, whether it's their first time or a repeat journey through. Working the steps the first time can feel scary or unfamiliar while also necessary, and we take this knowledge into consideration. We also recognize that for most of us committed to a twelve-step path, the steps are not meant to be worked through only once. Some steps you may practice on a day-to-day basis, while others may require a more thorough revisit at different times in your recovery. Many folks in long-term recovery make this a yearly practice, or whenever life challenges seem to necessitate reworking the steps.

This workbook is the first of its kind to have trauma as the focus alongside recovery principles in working the twelve steps. Our working definition of *trauma* is any unhealed wound—physical, emotional, sexual, spiritual, or otherwise—that gets in the way of you living the fullest life possible. As explored more fully in *Trauma and the 12 Steps* and in other resources we make available to you online, unhealed trauma is more than just diagnosable post-traumatic stress disorder. Innovations in the fields of medicine, psychology, counseling, social work, and addiction counseling continue to reveal that unhealed trauma is a major factor in the development of

---

* Jamie Marich, *Trauma and the 12 Steps: An Inclusive Guide to Enhancing Recovery* (Berkeley, CA: North Atlantic Books, 2020), 89.

addiction—as well as the potential for relapse. This understanding may challenge what you've originally been taught as a person in twelve-step recovery—that addiction is a primary disease. Period.

While some people see twelve-step programming and working the twelve steps as an antiquated practice, the position of Jamie and others who support her in the *Trauma and the 12 Steps* work is that the steps can still be incredibly useful. However, the flexibility inherent in the language must be harnessed if unhealed trauma is still present. Working the steps can be a valuable part of both initial and ongoing recovery as long as the role of unhealed trauma is acknowledged and honored. We've heard countless horror stories of people who were scared or otherwise shamed away from working the steps because their sponsors, professionals, or other guides wouldn't make modifications or meet them where they *were at* in the recovery process. We hope to change some of the rigid and often stifling mentality around step work with the approach we present in this workbook.

A hallmark of trauma-informed care is that trauma-responsive modifications may be necessary. For instance, while step-related tasks may need to be accepted with commitment, they do not have to be completed in perfect lockstep with traditional approaches or forms. This rigid thinking is what blocks many folks from even approaching the steps to begin with. As an early recovery friend of Jamie's wisely declared, "Your first time through, work the steps as best as you can."

We believe that applies for any venture you take through the steps at whatever place in life you find yourself. We invite you to make a commitment to do this trauma-informed work, appreciating its importance in empowering you with a sense of flexible structure you may need for successful recovery. You can bring in outside skills like meditation or non–twelve-step–specific coping strategies to help you meet the challenges that may come up in your body, mind, and spirit as you approach step work. Unhealed trauma is stored in the place in the brain that makes trauma-influenced reactions likely to play out in your body. Symptoms like tightening stomach and chest, sweaty palms, and a sense of checking out or shutting down can be common when you are faced with a task such as working the steps. The internal experiences that come up in working the steps may remind you of traumatic experiences or show you areas you still need to address and heal.

This is why we include a meditation and/or coping skill strategy of focus with each step. Being able to ground yourself and retreat if you become overwhelmed, especially if you are working through these steps on your own, is very important. If you ever become too overwhelmed in working any one step, know that you can take a break at any time. The opening exercise we offer in this workbook before you even work a single step is to take an inventory of your grounding, retreat, and safeguard strategies. We hope that using these will empower you to take the necessary breaks you need to feel stronger and more grounded so you can return to the work ahead.

If you have the ability to use this workbook alongside a sponsor or study group, that is ideal. Being able to share your step work with someone can be a big part of the healing process, as long as that person reasonably understands your need to take a more trauma-focused approach as advocated for in this workbook. You can also bring in other literature when working the steps. Each step in this workbook contains an excerpt from *Trauma and the 12 Steps* that you can use to further explore the step. As an alternative, you may choose to read the step you are working on in the book *Twelve Steps and Twelve Traditions** every day you are in progress with the step, meditate upon it, and then write a reflection. Another resource we now have available is *Trauma and the 12 Steps: Daily Meditations and Reflections,*[†] where readings for each day of every month correspond with each step. You may find these meditations supportive in your step work process. And always remember that there is no shame in seeking outside professional help. Some of the most successful step work we've seen people do and have had the privilege to witness ourselves has been in concert with professional trauma-focused therapy or support services.

Ready to prepare for the journey?

If so, let's begin!

> To visit a collection of online videos prepared by Jamie and her team that can support you in this work and its invitations, please visit:
> www.traumamadesimple.com

---

* Anonymous, *Twelve Steps and Twelve Traditions* (New York: Alcoholics Anonymous World Services, Inc., 1942/2004).

[†] Jamie Marich and Stephen Dansiger, *Trauma and the 12 Steps: Daily Meditations and Reflections* (Warren, OH: Creative Mindfulness Media, 2020).

The Original Twelve Steps of Alcoholics Anonymous

1. We admitted we were powerless over alcohol*—that our lives had become unmanageable.

2. Came to believe that a Power greater than ourselves could restore us to sanity.

3. Made a decision to turn our will and our lives over to the care of God as we understood Him.†

4. Made a searching and fearless moral inventory of ourselves.

5. Admitted to God, to ourselves, and to another human being the exact nature of our wrongs.

6. Were entirely ready to have God remove all these defects of character.

7. Humbly asked Him to remove our shortcomings.

8. Made a list of all persons we had harmed, and became willing to make amends to them all.

9. Made direct amends to such people wherever possible, except when to do so would injure them or others.

10. Continued to take personal inventory and when we were wrong promptly admitted it.

11. Sought through prayer and meditation to improve our conscious contact with God as we understood Him, praying only for knowledge of His will for us and the power to carry that out.

12. Having had a spiritual awakening as the result of these steps, we tried to carry this message to alcoholics‡ and to practice these principles in all our affairs.

---

* Feel free to replace this word with whatever feels appropriate to your recovery journey. We are flexible and invite you to be as well!

† Make any adjustments you need to make for gender or spiritual language. We embrace an inclusive approach to how you use pronouns and identifiers around *Higher Power. She, them,* or any other proper name is welcome. You may also use a word or a concept other than *God.* For instance, instead of *God* or *Higher Power,* many people use *Inner Power* or use the collective of the group as their inspiration.

‡ Feel free to replace this word with whatever feels appropriate to your recovery journey. We are flexible and invite you to be as well!

Step 0

Opening Self-Care Inventory

Grounding is the process of using any available sense or experience to return to the "here and now" if you've wandered away, or to stay in the here and now if that is your intention. Grounding prepares the base. Retreat is when you deliberately check in with that base to pause and to rest when you become overwhelmed. Retreat can be a safety net when you do work as involved as the twelve steps, yet also consider how leaning on the support of others can also be part of this safety planning. There is no right way to have grounding, retreat, and safety strategies in place, as long as you have them in place.

—Jamie

Grounding seems like a big task for many people in early recovery. In my instructions for grounding meditation, I always suggest if you're not able to find a sense of ground, then see if you can notice that with as little judgment as possible. This is the essence of what we're trying to do—reduce judgment of ourselves and of things, ground ourselves as deeply as we are able to in that moment, lean into that ground when necessary. Then we have a place of retreat and refuge, which is where we can find the deepest level of safety that we are able to find for today.

—Steve

List some of your favorite or "go-to" strategies for *grounding*. If you don't believe you have many or any at this point, don't worry, the opening meditation for Step One is focused on grounding.

As one of Steve's sponsors challenged him to do, write down one hundred things that make you feel good that do *not* involve drugs, alcohol, or acting out. One hundred sounds like a lot, so think small to start! Some examples include the minty-fresh feeling after you brush your teeth or the potentially pleasant sensation when you rub your eyes in the morning. This exercise may require more than one sitting. You can come back to this page throughout your step work and keep adding. Consider which of these activities can work for you as a refuge or a break if you need to take a pause when doing step work. As Steve's sponsor said, when things are feeling down or difficult, go to the list.

1. _____
2. _____
3. _____
4. _____
5. _____
6. _____
7. _____
8. _____
9. _____
10. _____
11. _____
12. _____
13. _____
14. _____
15. _____
16. _____
17. _____
18. _____
19. _____
20. _____
21. _____
22. _____
23. _____
24. _____
25. _____
26. _____
27. _____
28. _____
29. _____
30. _____
31. _____
32. _____
33. _____
34. _____
35. _____
36. _____
37. _____
38. _____
39. _____
40. _____
41. _____
42. _____
43. _____
44. _____
45. _____
46. _____
47. _____
48. _____
49. _____
50. _____
51. _____
52. _____
53. _____
54. _____
55. _____
56. _____
57. _____
58. _____
59. _____
60. _____
61. _____
62. _____
63. _____
64. _____
65. _____
66. _____
67. _____
68. _____
69. _____
70. _____
71. _____
72. _____
73. _____
74. _____
75. _____
76. _____
77. _____
78. _____
79. _____
80. _____
81. _____
82. _____
83. _____
84. _____
85. _____
86. _____
87. _____
88. _____
89. _____
90. _____
91. _____
92. _____
93. _____
94. _____
95. _____
96. _____
97. _____
98. _____
99. _____
100. _____

Safety may feel like a foreign idea to you at this point in your recovery. Remember that there may never be such a thing as feeling perfectly safe. Think in terms of *safe enough*. At this point in your recovery, are there any people with whom you feel *safe enough* who can offer support as you do this step work? Perhaps people don't feel especially safe to you right now—are there animals, places, or experiences that are fundamentally healthy, do not involve drugs, alcohol, or acting out, and feel safe enough? Consider whether any of these people, beings, places, or experiences can work for you as a refuge or a break when step work is getting overwhelming. We've deliberately made this an open space without lines so that if artwork feels more organic to you than writing, you may express yourself in that way.

Step 1

We admitted we were powerless over alcohol/our addiction,* that our lives had become unmanageable.

Spitting out my last drink was how I worked my First Step. In my attempts to get sober in the months before, I tried writing it out or talking it out. I tried looking at myself in the mirror like an after-school special, saying, "Jamie, you are powerless." In the days before that last drink I was caught in the trap again—trying to convince myself that I wasn't really an alcoholic. That I was just young. The truth was that I was tired. I felt like I was ready to just die and give up. So when my body rejected that last sip of wine and literally wouldn't let me swallow it, I knew I was done. My body worked the First Step for me and I was ready to do anything, literally anything my sponsor suggested at that point.

—Jamie

I tried to stop only with the help of my girlfriend for almost two years. At the very end, I had successfully not drunk (again) for almost two weeks. I was sitting at a bar and made the decision (again) to have just one. I went through my entire cycle that usually took a night of drinking in only three beers. First, I relaxed. Second, I became the lampshade guy. Third, I became deeply suicidal. I truly knew then that I could not go on in the same way.

—Steve

---

* You can insert whatever substance, behavior, or concept works best for you here.

BASIC GROUNDING MEDITATION

Grounding is a relative term. Much like perfect safety is a big ask for anyone in recovery, a perfect sense of grounding is often elusive, and may well be unrealistic. Demanding it of ourselves can be a motivation killer or a setup for failure. In this meditation, we seek to become *grounded enough* for this moment, for this day. The more we notice our level of grounding on a day-to-day basis, the more we will become attuned to what works best for us to ground ourselves more consistently. In the spirit of modification, you may elect to use a word other than grounding, such as *anchoring* or *settling* as your inspiration and guide for the meditation. Try this meditation and notice how it feels prior to starting, during the meditation, and when it ends.

- First, take a posture that feels sustainable for the amount of time you have scheduled for this meditation.

- Notice contact points. If you are seated in a chair, for instance, notice the sensation of your back against the chair. Notice the feeling in your seat, the backs of your legs, your feet on the floor.

- Notice other contact points, like your arms against your body, and your hands wherever they rest.

- Notice if one or more of these points of contact feels grounded, or more grounded than the others. If what you notice is, "I don't feel particularly grounded," then see if you can notice that lack of grounding with as little judgment as possible. If, in fact, you do feel some grounding somewhere, go ahead and lean into that grounding. Let yourself have that ground.

- For the remainder of this meditation, allow yourself to continue to lean into that ground. If anything changes during the meditation, let yourself notice it and move with it if necessary. Reground yourself at any time.

- Here, we are looking not for quantity, but rather for consistency in practice. Five minutes a day is just fine, and if five minutes is too long, one minute is just fine. The key is to practice daily or as consistently as possible. That's how we set up the habit of noticing where we are with our sense of grounding each day, and develop a better idea of what we need to do to ground ourselves proactively. Again, five minutes a day is even better than thirty minutes on Saturday with nothing at all the rest of the week.

Take a look at how Step One is worded, particularly the words *powerless* and *unmanageable.* Are these words you can relate to in the present, or are they triggering or shaming because of certain aspects of your history? All responses are valid and you may use this space to freewrite.

While many survivors and otherwise resistant people struggle with the term powerless, the step does not say that we are powerless people. The step simply says that we are powerless when it comes to alcohol, drugs, etc. This means that if we put alcohol or drugs into our body, they will win every time. Behaviors can have a similar impact. By admitting defeat, we are carving the pathway to reclaim our power on the road ahead. The distinction is an important one in working with newcomers or new clients who may feel disheartened or even shamed by words like powerless or unmanageable.*

Taking this passage into consideration, where are you able to see, identify, and/or admit *powerlessness* today? What about *unmanageability*?

---

* Jamie Marich, *Trauma and the 12 Steps: An Inclusive Guide to Enhancing Recovery*, 60.

If this is your first time working Step One, what prompts you to begin this journey *now*? Consider "going with" that question in an open-ended way and notice whatever comes up. You may end up working a lot of what needs to be done by letting yourself just riff! If you've worked this step before, or work it every day on some level (perhaps as part of your prayers, meditations, or self-talk), what is your focus in this current pass through the steps? What is the intention you are setting for how you would like your life to be different by working the step?

EXPRESSIVE ARTS OPTION: If freewriting alone on Step One does not feel sufficient, is there a way you can bring in another expressive practice (e.g., visual art, fiction, or poetry writing, playlist construction, songwriting, dancing, or acting out a dramatic scene—even if it's something as simple as making a gesture or series of gestures that reflects what this step means to you at this point in your journey)? As a reminder, you may use a separate journal or other media for this process.

Using freewriting or an expressive arts practice of your choice, reflect on what gratitude you may be noticing related to Step One and any thoughts, feelings, or sensations about your readiness to move to Step Two. Is there anything you may need to further prepare yourself for going on to the next step? Feel free to consult your "Step Zero" self-care inventory as a reference.

Step 2

Came to believe that a Power greater than ourselves could restore us to sanity.

I struggled a bit with the word sanity as it relates to Step Two. In all likelihood, this struggle originated in a belief I had before meeting my sponsor that I was just "crazy"... that my brain was broken beyond repair. That I was plagued with the same afflictions that seemed responsible for others in my family line treating me poorly. When I was able to approach sanity simply as a state of best possible health, it completely changed my relationship with this step.

—Jamie

Many times during the course of working the steps you may be instructed to go back to Step One. That was rarely the case for me. I was always told to go back to Step Two. One reason for that—I have been consistently convinced about the truth of Step One. My sponsors claimed their suggestion was a response to my deep belief that everyone else was salvageable, while there was no power external or internal that could ever help me to feel better. They suggested that my primary "insanity" was my view of myself as a lost cause. My Second Step only needed to be enough of a belief to keep going, keep using the power of the program, stay in contact with the people in it, and utilize my outside helpers. Eventually, they said, possibly quickly, possibly slowly, I would witness my own power.

—Steve

MEDITATION: BEFRIENDING YOUR BREATH

Our breath is our life force moving and dancing through us. Learning to take a deep, attentive breath during moments of stress or activation is one of the best stress-reducing practices that any human being can embrace. This practice becomes especially necessary for people on a recovery path and survivors of trauma. Our tendency can be to hold our breath, something that we likely developed by spending too much time in a state of hypervigilance.

To test out this contention, we invite you to crunch your shoulders up toward your ears for just a few moments. When we are in hypervigilance, our shoulders can assume this position of high alert. Now notice what's happening to your breath when your shoulders are up against your ears like this. It's very likely that your breath is shallow and you feel cut off from it. Now go ahead and release the shoulders and immediately notice what happens to your breath. Say hello to it if you like!

Engaging in specialty deep breathing exercises that you may learn in a yoga class or via online videos can be helpful yet challenging to those of us affected by trauma, especially if we feel cut off from our breath and our bodies. (We encourage you to check out our wide array of breath strategies at www.traumamadesimple.com.) In this meditation you are encouraged to start in a very slow and basic way. The intention here is to get to know your breath (hopefully you've already said hello to it) and begin paying attention to it.

- ◆ You may close your eyes, leave them open, or experiment with the two. Whichever position will help you feel safe enough yet stay engaged with the practice is optimal.

- ◆ Engage in the shoulder crunch and release at least three more times. Every time you release, try to pay a little more attention to how your breath responds to the release.

- ◆ Move into at least thirty seconds of just noticing the breath as it naturally rises and falls in your body. You do not have to do anything special with technique, simply notice. Does your breath feel warm, cool, or neutral moving through your body? Is there a sensation or even a sound that goes along with it? If you'd like to spend longer than thirty seconds in this practice, go for it.

- ◆ You may notice that your mind starts to wander as you begin and continue with the meditation. This is normal! Instead of judging yourself for not being able to pay attention, see if you can invite the attention back to the breath when you notice it wandering. Even if you have to do this every other second, truly, it's okay.

- Some people find it helpful to hold a grounding or anchoring object in their hand while they try this exercise (e.g., a rock, a recovery coin), and others find it helpful to focus on one part of the body and think about the breath moving in and out through that part of the body.

- Another favorite anchoring device of ours, drawing directly on wisdom from Buddha, is to repeat this saying as you breathe: "As I breathe in, I know I am breathing in. As I breathe out, I know I am breathing out." You can simply modify this to "In" (as you breathe in) and "Out" (as you breathe out).

- Try this exercise as many times as you need to get the flow of it and consider repeating it for consistency every day. If you find yourself stuck while working a step, put the pen aside and come back to the breath. Holding your breath does not make things easier! Your breath is your friend and wants to support you in this process of healing.

Take a look at how Step Two is worded, particularly the word *sanity* and the concept of *Power greater than ourselves*. Are these words and concepts that work for you in the present, or are they triggering or shaming because of certain aspects of your history? All responses are valid in this invitation to freewrite.

A great struggle with this step is the element of spirituality it introduces, even for those newcomers to twelve-step programming who do not identify unresolved trauma as a major issue. However, if a trauma survivor relied on the fight of self-sufficiency to get through the trauma and cope over the years, it may be very difficult for them to accept (at first) that something outside of themselves is going to help them heal from the addiction. Even if the individual believes in God and is open to spirituality, reliance on something other than self may be problematic for a trauma survivor. The word sanity also poses an interesting challenge. If we need to be "restored to sanity," then we must be insane! If a newcomer, especially a trauma survivor, reads this step without having the root meanings of insanity and sanity properly explained or at least explored, there is a greater risk for insult-induced triggering that can happen.*

Validating all of these as possible areas of struggle, where are you able to see, identify, or even admit areas in your life that are *unhealthy* today? Make it easier on yourself and use this word *(unhealthy)* for now! Where are you at with the concept of a *Higher Power* today (knowing that you have complete permission from us to use whatever may feel appropriate as a *Higher Power*—or a popular alternative, an *Inner Power*)? To really work this step you may have to do some venting, and that is okay.

---

* Jamie Marich, *Trauma and the 12 Steps: An Inclusive Guide to Enhancing Recovery*, 81–82.

If this is your first time working Step Two, what is prompting you to take this journey to the next level *now?* Consider "going with" that question in an open-ended way and notice whatever comes up. Remember, you have complete permission to vent. If you've worked this step before, or work it every day on some level (perhaps as part of your prayers, meditations, or self-talk), what is your focus in this pass through the steps? What is the intention you are setting for how you would like your life to be different by working the step?

EXPRESSIVE ARTS OPTION: If freewriting alone on Step Two does not feel sufficient, is there a way you can bring in another expressive practice (e.g., visual art, fiction, or poetry writing, playlist construction, songwriting, dancing, or acting out a dramatic scene—even if it's something as simple as making a gesture or series of gestures that reflects what this step means to you at this point in your journey)? As a reminder, you may use a separate journal or other media for this process.

Using freewriting or an expressive arts practice of your choice, reflect on what gratitude you may be noticing for Step Two and any thoughts, feelings, or sensations about your readiness to move to Step Three. Is there anything you may need to further prepare yourself for going on to the next step? Feel free to consult your "Step Zero" self-care inventory as a reference.

Step 3

—————

Made a decision to turn our will and our lives over to the care of God as we understood Him.*

*Allow me to personally and directly address the footnote we are putting on Step Three. Footnotes will appear throughout the workbook in several other places when using gendered language, especially for God or another spiritual entity. Truly, use whatever language, or for that matter gender (or nongender) you need here. Although I grew up with a very masculine concept of God, my recovery received a boost several years back when—at Steve's suggestion—I took out most masculine language when referring to my Higher Power and began primarily using the language of Divine Mother. For me, God, spiritual abuse, and the patriarchy were all rolled into one, as were pervasive messages that God was out to get me if I didn't behave. So, this step has historically been a minefield for me. Yet with all of that, it's still one of my favorites as very few things give me the level of peace as surrendering what is not in my control. If the God or Higher Power stuff is tricky for you, perhaps consider framing Step Three in this way.

—Jamie

At the end of the Third Step chapter of Twelve Steps and Twelve Traditions, Bill Wilson made a distinction that changed my life. He clarified that powerlessness is a doorway into the process, mostly related specifically to our addictive behaviors, and that we need all sorts of willpower to work the rest of these steps. Making a decision about anything takes willpower. Therefore, we are empowered by Step Three. We are not floppy-fish powerless and handing ourselves over blindly. We are bringing our own power into alignment with whatever Higher Power means to us, however that Power manifests. Then, from that alignment, we go out and think, speak, and act in the world.

—Steve

MEDITATION: HIGHER OR INNER POWER VISUALIZATION

On the twelve-step path you have complete freedom to choose or to allow your own conceptualization of a *Higher Power* to emerge. This includes not even needing to use the term *Higher Power*. For instance, many yogis prefer to use the term *Inner Power*, which feels more aligned with the belief that God, spirit, or anything Divine lives within you. God does not have to be some scary being up on a cloud looking over all of us. Yet, if you draw healthy and helpful comfort from that image of a God who hangs out on a cloud, you are completely empowered to use that image. If you identify as someone who is atheist or agnostic, what you use as a power greater than yourself (or outside of yourself) may look and feel completely different. In this meditation, you are given the freedom to explore.

- Begin by coming into at least thirty seconds of mindful breathing with your eyes closed or opened. Do whatever you may need to in order to feel supported and grounded before engaging in breath.

- Set an intention to work with the essence of Step Three for this meditation and ask yourself, through the breath, what needs to be revealed. Begin by asking which terminology may work best for you: *God, Higher Power, Inner Power, spirit, the universe, humankind, the Greater Good*, or something completely different. Notice what is revealed without forcing it and learn to listen to that vital spark that says, "This is it!" You will likely know it if you feel it. If nothing particularly resonates for you the first time, that's okay too. You can always try this as many times as you need to.

◆ After the term that works for you reveals itself, spend at least thirty seconds (longer if you wish) reflecting on it. With every breath, connect to it. Begin noticing how the body feels.

◆ Notice if anything emerges visually. The less you force it, the more likely your connection will happen. There are so many combinations of what may be revealed as viable for you. For some people the visual that shows up looks like a person or group of people, for others it's more like a light or even a sensation. Once again, if nothing special seems to happen, keep trying the exercise a few more times without forcing.

◆ Quick reminder: You cannot do anything wrong here! This may mean that you need to intentionally send away any old pictures or conceptualizations of what you were taught *God* or *Higher Power* needed to look like. You can literally shake it off or flick your hands to the ground in release.

◆ Whenever you see or sense into what is revealed, spend as much time as you need noticing it without judgment. Notice what happens in your breath. Notice what happens to your body. Notice if the experience is pleasant, unpleasant, or neutral.

◆ Pay attention and see if whatever you are noticing has a message for you, whether that comes in the forms of words or bodily sensations.

◆ Know that you can stop this meditation whenever you need to; you are in control the whole time. When it concludes, you may consider journaling or reaching out to a member of your support network if you need to further process the experience. If what emerged for you feels like it will work as you move forward with Step Three and the rest of the steps, we encourage you to go with it.

Take a look at how Step Three is worded, particularly the phrase *God as we understood Him*[*] and the concept of turning your will and your life over, really to anything. Are these phrases and concepts that work for you in the present, or are they triggering or shaming because of certain aspects of your history? All responses are valid. You have complete permission here to explore your understanding, as suggested by this step.

_____

[*] See page 27 for language modification suggestions.

Although some twelve-step groups and sponsors may misinterpret the step, in its truest form the step leaves it up to individuals to decide how they will conceptualize their Higher Power—an idea that allows for flexibility and modification. . . . For some, having the religious and spiritual elements downplayed or not even used may be part of the solution. For others, truly feeling free to develop a new relationship with spirituality or even religion may be the key to freedom. Remember that the program does allow people to find their own conceptualization of God, Higher Power, or as one of my teachers offers as an alternative, Inner Power.*

Even though the step references God, you are completely free to define *God/Higher Power/ Inner Power* or any alternative concept as you see fit. This may fly in the face of how you were raised or feel like it's egotistical for you to do the defining. Your self-esteem could also feel so low right now that you're filled with ideas that anything you conceptualize cannot possibly be good. See if you can set all of this aside and simply riff on how you need to conceptualize *God/Higher Power,* etc. in a way that works for you and your recovery today.

---

* Jamie Marich, *Trauma and the 12 Steps: An Inclusive Guide to Enhancing Recovery,* 61, 222.

If this is your first time working Step Three, what is prompting you to take this journey to the next level *now*? Consider "going with" that question in an open-ended way and notice whatever comes up. Remember, you have complete permission to explore and get creative. If you've worked this step before, or work it every day on some level (perhaps as part of your prayers, meditations, or self-talk), what is your focus in this pass through the steps? What is the intention you are setting for how you would like your life to be different by working this step?

EXPRESSIVE ARTS OPTION: If freewriting alone on Step Three does not feel sufficient, is there a way you can bring in another expressive practice (e.g., visual art, fiction or poetry writing, playlist construction, songwriting, dancing, or acting out a dramatic scene—even if it's something as simple as making a gesture or series of gestures that reflects what this step means to you at this point in your journey)? As a reminder, you may use a separate journal or other media for this process.

Using freewriting or an expressive arts practice of your choice, reflect on what gratitude you may be noticing for Step Three and any thoughts, feelings, or sensations about your readiness to move to Step Four. Is there anything you may need to further prepare yourself for going on to the next step? Feel free to consult your "Step Zero" self-care inventory as a reference.

Step 4

Made a searching and fearless moral inventory of ourselves.

Taking inventories ought not turn into exercises in shaming. I am forever grateful that Janet (my first sponsor) gave me complete permission to take stock of the good stuff about me and my character as well, which included identifying areas of my own creativity and spirit that helped me to survive. There are so many ways that one can honestly take stock without turning Step Four into an exercise in shame and self-hatred. The key here is, are you willing to take an honest look at yourself and how you respond to the world?

—Jamie

My first sponsor Randy had a one-page-long inventory. My own first inventory was over thirty pages long. The woman who Twelfth-Stepped me, Maggie, hers was the length of a novel, or at least I have to believe her after she showed me the giant stack of paper she claimed to be her Fourth Step. Regardless of length, I have found it is critical to let people know you are working on Step Four, whether it be a sponsor, a therapist, a friend, or a community of friends. We are looking in depth at some difficult truths, some of which were driven by or are manifestations of our traumas and adverse life events. We need to nurture ourselves through this process. Many people have faltered at this step because they were not surrounded by trauma-informed others. I provided myself with the people and environments I needed to do this step safely and effectively. You can too.

—Steve

MEDITATION: LOVING KINDNESS

In the world of mindfulness, Loving Kindness meditation has become one of the most popular ways to engage in heart practice. As we work Step Four, it is critical that we counterbalance the pain and distress of looking at our history of trauma and adverse life events with the resources and resilience it takes to keep going. Loving Kindness meditation allows us to keep a focus on (and to cultivate) loving kindness toward ourselves and toward others. This quality of loving kindness in and of itself is known to be a dedicated result of working the steps and other spiritual paths. However, years of experience have shown that in order to work the steps, it helps to actively cultivate these heart qualities, even if we don't fully feel them at first. Here is how you might practice loving kindness as you enter and progress through Step Four and later steps.

- First, take a posture that feels sustainable for the amount of time you have scheduled for this meditation.

- Notice contact points. If you are seated in a chair for instance, notice the sensation of your back against the chair. Notice the feeling in your seat, the backs of your legs, your feet on the floor.

- Notice other contact points, like your arms against your body, and your hands wherever they rest.

- Notice if one or more of these points of contact feels grounded or more grounded than the others. If what you notice is, "I don't feel particularly grounded," then see if you can notice that lack of grounding with as little judgment as possible. If, in fact, you do feel some grounding somewhere, go ahead and lean into that grounding. Let yourself have that grounding.

- Begin to silently repeat the loving kindness phrases included here, or feel free to use others that you find or create yourself. Repeat these toward yourself first: *May I be free from fear; May I be healthy (or healed); May I be happy; May I be at ease.* You can start with three rounds of these phrases for each person or being you are sending them to.

- Now begin emanating these phrases outward as far as you please. You might start with someone it is easy to send loving kindness to, like a loved one or a pet. *May you be free from fear; May you be healthy; May you be happy; May you be at ease.* You might also send it to someone who has been a great help to you. You can then move outward incrementally, sending it to everyone on your block, everyone in your city, your country, this world, even as far as all beings in all known and unknown universes. For the last round, consider sending one more set of these phrases back toward yourself.

◆ Know that in traditional Loving Kindness meditation, we often will send loving kindness toward a person or being we call "the difficult person." In this version of the meditation, that is not required, as we are trying to build our positive neural networks, rather than challenge ourselves in this way from the beginning. However, as you progress through working with this meditation and Step Four, you can consider adding the difficult person to your meditation. Often the order is something like: ourselves, the easy person, the person who has helped you, the neutral person, and finally, the difficult person. Then you can proceed with sending it further and wider, as before.

◆ As with other meditations, we are looking here not for quantity, but rather for consistency of practice. Five minutes is just fine, and if five minutes is too long, one minute is just fine. The key is to practice daily if possible. That's how we establish the habit of working with loving kindness each day. Again, five minutes a day is even better than thirty minutes on Saturday with nothing at all the rest of the week.

Take a look at how Step Four is worded, particularly the word *moral,* which is a stumbling block for many of us. What is your present association with the word *moral* and how might this keep you stuck in approaching the step? Consider looking up the word *moral* and its various meanings in the dictionary—pick the presentation of it that works best for you and then see if you can approach this step from there.

Steps Four and Five in a twelve-step program are no doubt the gauntlet, for these steps ask us to make an inventory of our rights and wrongs (preferably in writing), and then share these findings with another human being. . . . Many individuals struggle with the word moral, especially if they grew up in religious environments; or they automatically associate the word immoral with the idea that they are defective. People need proper guidance to do this step in a sensitive manner. *

Step Four should never be a punishment, rather it is an opportunity to take stock—a natural extension of what may have led us to approach this program or work a Step One in the first place. If I can reword and thus rethink this step as *taking stock* of the things I see about myself, both healthy/unhealthy and everything in between, might that ease some of the anxiety around the concept of *moral inventory?*

---

* Jamie Marich, *Trauma and the 12 Steps: An Inclusive Guide to Enhancing Recovery,* 83.

If this is your first time working Step Four, what is prompting you to take this journey to the next level *now?* Consider "going with" that question in an open-ended way and notice whatever comes up. Let it naturally lead you into the inventory, "taking stock," or whatever phrase you need to use to get this step done. Remember the wisdom of Jamie's friend—do your best to work the step as you can right now in your journey. It doesn't have to be perfect. If you've worked this step before, what is your focus in this pass through the steps? What is the intention you are setting for how you would like your life to be different by working this step?

EXPRESSIVE ARTS OPTION: If freewriting alone on Step Four does not feel sufficient, is there a way you can bring in another expressive practice (e.g., visual art, fiction or poetry writing, playlist construction, songwriting, dancing, or acting out a dramatic scene—even if it's something as simple as making a gesture or series of gestures that reflects what the step means to you at this point in your journey)? As a reminder, you may use a separate journal or other media for this process.

Using freewriting or an expressive arts practice of your choice, reflect on what gratitude you may be noticing for Step Four and any thoughts, feelings, or sensations about your readiness to move to Step Five. Is there anything you may need to further prepare yourself for going on to the next step? Feel free to consult your "Step Zero" self-care inventory as a reference.

Step 5

Admitted to God,* to ourselves, and to another human being the exact nature of our wrongs.

Saying something out loud can diffuse its power to control me—that is the complete wonder of this step in my life. Even though I worked my first several Fifth Steps with pastoral figures, over the years I've gone on to share Fifth Steps or Fifth Step variations with a variety of caring recovery family members and healers. There is so much truth to that idea, now intoned by many in the healing arts, that shame cannot exist when our stories are shared in safe places. For me, that is the essence of what Step Five can be.

—Jamie

My first Fifth Step with Randy will always be my template for what it means to share honestly with someone, and the results that honesty can provide. I had developed a trusting relationship with him. He had shown himself to care about my recovery, and he had taken time to show me that I was heard and seen. He also showed me boundaries though, like when I went to his midtown apartment for Step Five having carved out twelve hours for the exercise, and he said I had two hours to do our work before he went to the gym. In those two hours, the combination of trust, compassion, connection, and boundaries yielded what felt to me like a spiritual experience—sunlight was extra bright, the wind was crisper—I could sense I had changed somehow.

—Steve

---

* As a compassionate reminder, use of *God* or *Higher Power* language is not needed to work this step. You can use *Inner Power, the universe,* the collective of the group, anything that feels helpful in your process.

ADVANCED GROUNDING MEDITATION

People can never have too many methods at their disposal to practice grounding, especially when working Steps Four and Five, which are known to be overwhelming for people. Feeling overwhelmed can be a normal part of life in recovery, so working with finding one's ground in response to stressors that come up in this step can be excellent training for the journey ahead. Consider trying out some of these strategies for grounding, building on what we gave you in the meditation for Step One. Let the person who is hearing your Fifth Step know that you may need to take a "grounding break" every now and again as you share what you need to share. You can even invite them to remind you of your grounding skills if they notice that you are becoming too overwhelmed or even dissociated as you share. Remember that other words like anchoring and settling may be a better alternative to you than grounding. You may even describe this process to your sponsor or the person hearing your Fifth Step as needing to *catch your breath* or *take a break.*

- Take a look around the room or space where you currently find yourself and notice what you see. Observe and describe it, without getting too caught up in analyzing what you see. Perhaps you notice an object that especially resonates with you. Maybe it's a figurine, a clock, a picture, a statue, or a certain color pattern on a set of curtains.

- Designate that object or thing standing out to you as an *anchor object.* Whenever you feel shaky or are not sure where you are at, you can look at that anchor object and have assurance that you are here, now, and present.

- Continue this process of scanning with your other senses, especially if the visual anchor doesn't feel particularly strong. Notice what you hear in your space (or the absence of sound), and what you smell when you take a breath. Maybe there's a taste in your mouth.

- For the sense of touch or sensation, touch your clothes, press your feet into the floor, or make contact with your fingers and whatever surface on which you are sitting.

- Notice where you feel your sense of *here, now,* and *being in the present* the strongest, and practice returning here several times throughout your day, especially in advance of working Step Five.

Take a look at how Step Five is worded and notice where some problems may exist for you. The permissiveness that we've given you to alter the language and conceptualization around *God/ Higher Power* applies here too. Might there be past experiences with speaking something out loud to someone else that did not go well for you, and might that be a roadblock to you working Step Five at this point?

Nowhere does it say that the Fifth Step needs to be heard by a sponsor or a minister; it just needs to be heard by another human being. . . . Steps Four and Five are tricky. Often described as the hardest steps to get through, the gauntlet can prove to be especially challenging for those with unresolved trauma. Challenging, but not impossible—if proper preparation has taken place.[*]

You are empowered to choose the person who feels as safe and as affirming as possible, despite the fact that you may have been told that a pastoral figure or a sponsor must hear your Fifth Step. Trauma survivors often feel more comfortable sharing their Fifth Step with a professional, and this option is totally acceptable. Who is standing out in your life and your circle of support right now as the best possible candidate to hear what you came up with in Step Four?

---

[*] Jamie Marich, *Trauma and the 12 Steps: An Inclusive Guide to Enhancing Recovery*, 20, 84.

If this is your first time working Step Five, what is prompting you to take this journey to the next level *now*? Notice that drive and honor it as evidence you are moving in the right direction!

If you've worked this step before, what is your focus in this pass through the steps? What is the intention you are setting for how you would like your life to be different by working this step?

EXPRESSIVE ARTS OPTION: If freewriting alone on Step Five does not feel sufficient, is there a way you can bring in another expressive practice (e.g., visual art, fiction or poetry writing, playlist construction, songwriting, dancing, or acting out a dramatic scene—even if it's something as simple as making a gesture or series of gestures that reflects what this step means to you at this point in your journey)? As a reminder, you may use a separate journal or other media for this process.

Using freewriting or an expressive arts practice of your choice, reflect on what gratitude you may be noticing for Step Five and any thoughts, feelings, or sensations about your readiness to move on to Step Six. Is there anything you may need to further prepare yourself for going on to the next step? Feel free to consult your "Step Zero" self-care inventory as a reference.

Step 6

Were entirely ready to have God* remove all these defects of character.

This step has always been a challenge for me, as much as I've benefited from working it (together with Step Seven). My trauma left me with a clear belief that "I am defective," so some of my struggles were obvious. Fortunately, Janet and other great recovery mentors I've had over the years gave me complete permission to change the language around. I came to understand that these "defects" were simply the evidence of unhealed wounds from trauma that kept me unhealthy. In many cases, these "defects" kept me alive and functional in my childhood and in some cases during my drinking. In recovery I've learned they no longer work for me, and that taking this step is my way of acknowledging that reality.

—Jamie

Of all the verbiage in the program that was not trauma-informed when it was created in the pre–trauma theory 1930s, "defects of character" is at the forefront. I have always been fonder of the reference to "shortcomings" in the Seventh Step, which I was told simply meant coming up short of my best or higher self. That indicates a horizon to go toward as well as some trauma-informed gentleness. So, in this step, I seek to become entirely ready to walk steadily toward that horizon, bolstered by the first five steps and the support I have around me.

—Steve

---

* As a compassionate reminder, use of *God* or *Higher Power* language is not needed to work this step. You can use *Inner Power, the universe,* the collective of the group, anything that feels helpful in your process.

MEDITATION: MINDFULNESS OF BODY

One of our Zen teachers once said to a group of beginning meditators, "This is not actually a practice of the mind. It is a practice of the body." Allowing ourselves to become mindful of our body, which includes the breath, gives us an alternative to focusing in on our eternally moving mind and its gyrations. It allows for spaciousness in our thinking and emotions. Thus, the practice allows us to come into a humble relationship with ourselves, our strengths, and our shortcomings. It gives us the opportunity to sit with what is happening in the moment and listen to our innermost selves for what we need to accept and keep, and what we need to change.

- First, take a posture that feels sustainable for the amount of time you have scheduled for this meditation. If you choose to stand, lie down, or be in motion, that will work too.

- Notice contact points. If you are seated in a chair for instance, notice the sensation of your back against the chair. Notice the feeling in your seat, the backs of your legs, your feet on the floor.

- Notice other contact points, like your arms against your body, and your hands wherever they rest.

- Notice if one or more of these points of contact feels grounded, more grounded than the others. If what you notice is, "I don't feel particularly grounded," then see if you can notice that lack of grounding with as little judgment as possible. If, in fact, you do feel some grounding somewhere, go ahead and lean into that grounding. Let yourself have that grounding.

- You may continue to be aware of bodily sensations related to what you are noticing in this moment. We also invite you to direct some attention to your breath, which is a big part of mindfulness of the body. Notice the physical sensations just outside or just inside the nostrils, or the rising and the falling of the belly. Take a few breaths from this place.

- When your mind inevitably goes into thought, stop for a moment and notice you have left your object of meditation, the body and/or the breath. Note to yourself, *thinking*, and then return to your observation point. Whether you never have to do this again, or you do it a thousand times in five minutes, no matter—you are successfully working with mindfulness of the body.

- This simple practice can become your primary practice going forward if you like. Settle into your posture, notice the body, notice the breath, notice you have gone into thought and lost your awareness of body and breath, and return to the body and breath.

- As with other meditations, we are looking here not for quantity, but rather for a consistency of practice.

The wording in Step Six is rife with many potential problems; it is naturally the step where I most emphasize the need for modification. For instance, in the basic text of the Workaholics Anonymous fellowship, an allowance is made to replace character defect with negative coping skill. These generally develop as a result of unhealed trauma or wounding. The addictive substance or behavior of choice simply amplifies the behavioral evidence that the wound(s) in question manifests. [*]

How can you change the language around in a way that makes working this step more approachable? Some people prefer to see defects of character as negative or unhealthy coping skills that developed in response to unhealed or unaddressed wounding.

---

[*] Jamie Marich, *Trauma and the 12 Steps: An Inclusive Guide to Enhancing Recovery*, 85.

Using the language that you've determined works for you in the previous question, how can you more effectively approach this step? Sometimes we may not feel *ready*, another word used in this step, until we are adequately prepared. This can include making use of our support system, working coping skills or other strategies, or getting to the place we want to be spiritually.

If this is your first time working Step Six, what is prompting you to take this journey to the next level *now?* Flowing from the previous item, what preparations may you need to take in order to become *ready* for this process? If you've worked this step before, what is your focus in this pass through the steps? What is the intention you are setting for how you would like your life to be different by working this step?

EXPRESSIVE ARTS OPTION: If freewriting alone on Step Six does not feel sufficient, is there a way you can bring in another expressive practice (e.g., visual art, fiction or poetry writing, playlist construction, songwriting, dancing, or acting out a dramatic scene—even if it's something as simple as making a gesture or series of gestures that reflects what this step means to you at this point in your journey)? As a reminder, you may use a separate journal or other media for this process.

Using freewriting or an expressive arts practice of your choice, reflect on what gratitude you may be noticing for Step Six and any thoughts, feelings, or sensations about your readiness to move to Step Seven. Is there anything you may need to further prepare yourself for going on to the next step? Feel free to consult your "Step Zero" self-care inventory as a reference.

Step 7

___

Humbly asked Him* to remove our shortcomings.

As with any step, the language and implications of this can be loaded, especially if we've survived spiritual trauma or spiritual wounding. I've come to simplify Step Seven as such: I am willing to change, to work on myself, and I'm going to ask the God of my understanding to help with this process.

—*Jamie*

Before recovery, I thought humility had something to do with being a doormat. It didn't help when I heard the words "right-sized" in meetings and in the AA literature, which I equated with making myself as small as possible. The first six steps retooled my thinking on humility so that I could work Step Seven. Now I see humility as a deep sense of acceptance and gratitude for all the possibilities of recovery. It is a setting of intention to seek to speak and act compassionately and in the spirit of loving kindness as I navigate my days.

—*Steve*

___

* As a reminder, you can amend this language in any way you see fit.

MEDITATION: MINDFULNESS OF FEELING TONE

Mindfulness of Feeling Tone allows us to take our mindfulness of the body and expand it out to other elements of our being. The factor that provides containment and direction for this meditation is a rating system related to our experience. Think about it. Anything and everything we can think, feel, or experience, couldn't it all be rated on a scale of Pleasant, Unpleasant, or Neutral? That is what we do in this meditation. It helps to further build our distress tolerance, and it helps to give perspective to all of our experiences without judgment or shame. And it helps us to work Step Seven by noting our changing relationship to ourselves and our experiences, opening up the opportunity for a willingness to accept any help available to us and move further into humility with a foundation of dignity and power.

- First, take a posture that feels sustainable for the amount of time you have scheduled for this meditation. You may choose a nonseated posture.

- Notice contact points. If you are seated in a chair for instance, notice the sensation of your back against the chair. Notice the feeling in your seat, the backs of your legs, your feet on the floor.

- Notice other contact points, like your arms against your body, and your hands wherever they rest.

- Notice if one or more of these points of contact feels grounded, more grounded than the others. If what you notice is, "I don't feel particularly grounded," then see if you can notice that lack of grounding with as little judgment as possible. If you do feel some grounding somewhere, go ahead and lean into that grounding. Let yourself have that grounding.

- As you settle into your posture and breathing, notice whatever comes into your consciousness first. Is it a bodily sensation, an emotion, or a thought? As soon as you notice what you are noticing, take a breath and rate it on the scale of Pleasant, Unpleasant, or Neutral. Notice that experience and then return to your original object of meditation whether it is the body or the breath.

- As soon as you notice another thought, feeling, or sensation, take another moment and give it a rating. Simply continue this process as often as it arises for the duration of your meditation.

- When you finish the meditation, notice a general sense of Pleasant, Unpleasant, or Neutral. Notice anything that seems the same from before the meditation session, and anything that has changed.

- Each day we may build a little more distress tolerance, a little more ability to maintain perspective.

Take a look at how Step Seven is worded and notice where some problems may exist for you. You've done this now with several steps so hopefully the process is becoming familiar to you.

People often work Steps Six and Seven together, or very closely together. . . . In so much of the criticism about twelve-step recovery, many constantly circle back to this idea that twelve-step recovery places too much emphasis on character defects and humility, and not enough emphasis on empowerment. If a person with unresolved trauma has worked through the first five steps in a properly guided manner, hopefully these steps do not have to be as big of a gauntlet as Steps Four and Five. *

If you've teased out some of your doubts and problems with Step Six, hopefully these will translate into how you can approach and work Step Seven. How might you be finding that to be the case, as these steps are often worked together?

---

* Jamie Marich, *Trauma and the 12 Steps: An Inclusive Guide to Enhancing Recovery*, 84.

If this is your first time working Step Seven, what is prompting you to take this journey to the next level *now*? Are you noticing any stumbling blocks as you transition from Step Six to Step Seven? If you've worked this step before, what is your focus in this pass through the steps? What is the intention you are setting for how you would like your life to be different by working this step?

EXPRESSIVE ARTS OPTION: If freewriting alone on Step Seven does not feel sufficient, is there a way you can bring in another expressive practice (e.g., visual art, fiction or poetry writing, playlist construction, songwriting, dancing, or acting out a dramatic scene—even if it's something as simple as making a gesture or series of gestures that reflects what this step means to you at this point in your journey)? As a reminder, you may use a separate journal or other media for this process.

Using freewriting or an expressive arts practice of your choice, reflect on what gratitude you may be noticing for Step Seven and any thoughts, feelings, or sensations about your readiness to move to Step Eight. Is there anything you may need to further prepare yourself for going on to the next step? Feel free to consult your "Step Zero" self-care inventory as a reference.

Step 8

Made a list of all persons we had harmed, and became willing to make amends to them all.

The biggest problem I had with working this step is that there were people on my list who I also felt owed me amends. I could never have done Step Eight, or Step Nine, without the guidance of a sponsor who helped me to wade through all of these grey areas. I think people get tripped up with these steps because they may feel it's a black or white thing, and some of the sponsorship out there may promote that. The subtleties must be honored.

—Jamie

One of my sponsors had me make my list, and then as soon as it was finished, I was launched into the Ninth Step. When I was going through the steps a second time, a later sponsor had me make the list and then suggested I become willing to make amends to everyone on the list before moving into any amends. This gave me a wonderful idea for a trauma-informed way to work with others. I now suggest a collaborative effort between sponsor and sponsee to determine which method is a fit. This provides another empowering moment for the person working the steps. Trauma-sensitive empowerment heals.

—Steve

MEDITATION: MINDFULNESS OF MIND

Mindfulness of Mind takes us to another level of awareness of how our mind experiences things. Instead of a rating system, we are allowing ourselves to notice a bit more of what our mind is up to on a moment-to-moment basis. Noticing our mind as an Eighth Step exercise allows for a more integrated view of our mind, our body, and our past experiences in life. It helps us further train our mind to lean toward nonjudgment. That spirit of nonjudgment will more than likely transfer quite nicely to our upcoming journey into the world of forgiveness.

- First, take a posture that feels sustainable for the amount of time you have scheduled for this meditation. You may choose a nonseated posture. Eyes may be open or closed.

- Notice contact points. If you are seated in a chair for instance, notice the sensation of your back against the chair. Notice the feeling in your seat, the backs of your legs, your feet on the floor.

- Notice other contact points, like your arms against your body, and your hands wherever they rest.

- Notice if one or more of these points of contact feels grounded, more grounded than the others. If what you notice is, "I don't feel particularly grounded," then see if you can notice that lack of grounding with as little judgment as possible. If you do feel some grounding somewhere, go ahead and lean into that grounding. Let yourself have that grounding.

- After taking a number of breaths, notice what you are noticing. Allow your mind to identify the sensation or the experience, and then notice which of your senses has brought it to your attention. Is it a sound? A smell? A taste? Is it something you are seeing, regardless of whether your eyes are closed? Is it a bodily sensation, something from the world of touch? With this meditation, along with noticing the category of sense related to what you are aware of, notice whether you are inclined to go toward it or away from it, with as little judgment as possible. We are just noticing, not judging. Once you have investigated this part of your mind's experience, let go and go back to your breathing or body.

- Much like the Mindfulness of Feeling Tone meditation, continue this process for the length of the meditation. Unlike the Mindfulness of Feeling Tone meditation, allow yourself to take a few breaths in between each round of noticing what your mind is landing upon.

- As with other meditations, here we are looking not for quantity, but rather consistency. In these later steps, we are allowing ourselves to investigate more complex aspects of our experience and our mind. Be gentle with yourself if you find yourself taken away by thoughts. Your mind is just doing what it is built to do, it is thinking.

Take a look at how Step Eight is worded and notice where some problems may exist for you. You may have to explore the word *amends* (get out the dictionary, notice what you notice) or talk to others in your recovery circles to get their experience, strength, and hope on what it means to make amends.

Steps Eight and Nine, often referred to as the "making things right" steps, usher in their own unique set of challenges. With proper guidance and a productive working through of the previous seven steps, these paired amends steps do not have to be as scary as they seem. . . . Without proper guidance, working these steps can be a disaster for someone in recovery who has not fully addressed issues of unresolved trauma, especially if people on the amends list (Step Eight) are some of the same people who inflicted the trauma.*

Above all else, this step is about willingness—do you have the willingness to make things right if it's in the best interest of yourself and the person involved? To answer this question you and your sponsor or support system may need to explore what it means for you to be *willing*. Bear in mind that even willingness may come in degrees. For instance, you may be willing enough even if you don't feel completely ready to go there, and that may be okay for now. And the guidance you receive from a sponsor or professional may be that actually making the amends itself in Step Nine may not be in your best interest or in the best interest of others. Yet exploring the willingness component can still be therapeutic to your process.

If this is your first time working Step Eight, what is prompting you to take this journey to the next level *now*? If you've worked this step before, what is your focus in this pass through the steps? What is the intention you are setting for how you would like your life to be different by working this step?

---

* Jamie Marich, *Trauma and the 12 Steps: An Inclusive Guide to Enhancing Recovery*, 85–86.

EXPRESSIVE ARTS OPTION: If freewriting alone on Step Eight does not feel sufficient, is there a way you can bring in another expressive practice (e.g., visual art, fiction or poetry writing, playlist construction, songwriting, dancing, or acting out a dramatic scene—even if it's something as simple as making a gesture or series of gestures that reflects what this step means to you at this point in your journey)? As a reminder, you may use a separate journal or other media for this process.

Using freewriting or an expressive arts practice of your choice, reflect on what gratitude you may be noticing for Step Eight and any thoughts, feelings, or sensations about your readiness to move to Step Nine. Is there anything you may need to further prepare yourself for going on to the next step? Feel free to consult your "Step Zero" self-care inventory as a reference.

Step 9

———

Made direct amends to such people wherever possible except when to do so would injure them or others.

Once again, the guidance I received in working Step Nine was not only important for me working the step . . . it helped me to learn the sacred art of discernment. I know I have the tendency to sluff off making amends and justify it through this lens of injury to others, and that could just be me making an excuse. It could also be legitimate. This step was the first serious exercise I worked in helping me to know the difference.

—*Jamie*

I look at Step Nine the way that I look at loving kindness meditation. Throughout this step I come back to myself as one of the amends, one of those beings who needs my compassion. As I toggle between making amends to others and making amends to myself, the compassion, self-compassion, and appreciative joy grow. Equanimity can be the result of this step, especially if I honor the reciprocal healing that is in progress.

—*Steve*

MEDITATION: MINDFULNESS OF WISDOM

Adapted from an early Buddhist teaching called the Four Foundations of Mindfulness, Mindfulness of Wisdom can mean many things, including maintaining mindfulness of larger teachings. When applied to the twelve steps, there is so much we can draw from and meditate upon. While some of the twelve-step literature suffers from its time and place of origin and therefore is not trauma-informed, the reason twelve-step recovery has survived and thrived is because of the greater wisdom at its foundation and within it. We can utilize traditional twelve-step teachings for this meditation, or we can reach into the spiritual, psychological, and humanistic traditions over the millennia for more mindfulness-focused practice. We have come to the end of a process here in Steps Four through Nine, and as such, are ready to consider, be informed by, and enact the teachings as we go through our amends process.

- First, take a posture that feels sustainable for the amount of time you have scheduled for this meditation. You may choose a nonseated posture. Eyes may be open or closed.

- Notice contact points. If you are seated in a chair for instance, notice the sensation of your back against the chair. Notice the feeling in your seat, the backs of your legs, your feet on the floor.

- Notice other contact points, like your arms against your body, and your hands wherever they rest.

- Notice if one or more of these points of contact feels grounded, more grounded than the others. If what you notice is, "I don't feel particularly grounded," then see if you can notice that lack of grounding with as little judgment as possible. If you do feel some grounding somewhere, go ahead and lean into that grounding. Let yourself have that grounding.

- Choose one twelve-step teaching that you are going to investigate during this meditation period. You can simply make it a mantra to repeat over and again, or you can gently bring it into your consciousness and look at it from all sides.

- The teachings can include but are not limited to: *One day at a time, live and let live, easy does it,* or any other slogans; the twelve steps as a whole, or one of the individual steps, the power of fellowship, the essence of sponsorship, humility, willingness, gratitude, or any other of the dozens of teachings that have sprung from the twelve steps.

- You can always utilize another spiritual path's teachings as your object of meditation. In Buddhist practice for instance, meditating on loving kindness, compassion, sympathetic joy, and/or equanimity is a common practice. You can use anything that has arisen from your being in this program, whether it is spiritual, psychological, humanistic, atheistic—any teaching that resonates with you.

- Allow yourself as much as possible to bask in these teachings, to allow them to become further integrated into your life. As always, even with a more complex meditation such as this, just five minutes a day may be your best bet to establish consistent practice.

Take a look at how Step Nine is worded and notice where some problems may exist for you. There are many different opinions in twelve-step circles about whether you as the individual are included in the qualifier "except when to do so would injure them or others." Our vote is that yes, of course you are included.

If traumatized individuals have not yet taken sufficient steps to reprocess the trauma (either in twelve-step recovery or through professional counseling), the likelihood is very high that they will be emotionally ill-equipped to determine what constitutes harm to self or others in making amends. The greatest emotional disasters I have seen with people working Steps Eight and Nine are when they refuse to heed the guidance of a sponsor and/or counselor. I've seen many cases of people in recovery who have gone to abusive parents or an abusive spouse and dumped everything for the sake of making things right. Yet the other party may not have the emotional capacity to reason, especially if that other party is still inflicting trauma on others. Thus, further shaming can result from the process of doing Steps Eight and Nine, which is not the intention of the step. *

Whether or not we go on to make the direct amends, having the conversations with our sponsor or other guides in the process of determining how to make them (or whether to make them at all) is vital to our growth. What have you learned about the art of making living amends in this process, considering that the best amends we can make come in the form of changed behavior moving forward?

---

* Jamie Marich, *Trauma and the 12 Steps: An Inclusive Guide to Enhancing Recovery*, 86.

If this is your first time working Step Nine, what is prompting you to take this journey to the next level *now*? If you've worked this step before, what is your focus in this pass through the steps? What is the intention you are setting for how you would like your life to be different by working this step?

EXPRESSIVE ARTS OPTION: If freewriting alone on Step Nine does not feel sufficient, is there a way you can bring in another expressive practice (e.g., visual art, fiction or poetry writing, playlist construction, songwriting, dancing, or acting out a dramatic scene—even if it's something as simple as making a gesture or series of gestures that reflects what this step means to you at this point in your journey)? As a reminder, you may use a separate journal or other media for this process.

Using freewriting or an expressive arts practice of your choice, reflect on what gratitude you may be noticing for Step Nine and any thoughts, feelings, or sensations about your readiness to move to Step Ten. Is there anything you may need to further prepare yourself for going on to the next step? Feel free to consult your "Step Zero" self-care inventory as a reference.

Step 10

Continued to take personal inventory and when we were wrong promptly admitted it.

Working Step Ten on a consistent basis has taught me a great deal about the power of personal responsibility. It also teaches me where I have a tendency to spend so much energy fighting—fighting to prove that my opinion and perspective are right, even when they're clearly harming or impacting another. On so many occasions, being able to say "I was wrong, I'm going to let this go," has opened up a new pathway to peace.

—Jamie

Between working the steps and working on my recovery in general, by the time I reach the so-called maintenance Steps of Ten, Eleven, and Twelve, I am ready to walk this new path I have forged—consistently. Step Ten gives me a simple formula. All I need to do is stay self-aware, and when I am not as skillful as I want to be in my thought, speech, or actions, I can make amends as soon as possible and move on. As one of my roommates in early sobriety would say to me each morning before we headed out the door, "Okay! Let's go out there and not create any new Ninth Steps!"

—Steve

MEDITATION: DAILY PRACTICE LOG

The concept of inventory in the twelve steps directly translates to the concept of self-improvement or self-evaluation popular in other healing modalities, as well as to the observance of self-study in the yoga traditions. Many different methods can work for engaging in the practice of self-inventory, and Step Ten gives us an opportunity to explore and see what will work best for us. The key is to find a self-evaluation practice where we do not beat ourselves up over every little "wrongdoing" or slip in interaction or self-care, yet we stay consistent with regard to looking at ourselves and what works to help us stay as healthy as possible.

Jamie's first sponsor Janet once advised her to write a list of everything she was doing (or not doing) on the weeks when she felt the most solid in her recovery. Janet then advised her to leave this list in her Big Book or on the refrigerator, so during weeks that were a struggle she could go to this list and take stock. For your Step Ten practice, you may consider doing something as simple as that, especially if you've been living on a recovery path for a while. If you've not yet considered or tapped into what a good week feels like, you may consider engaging in this more specific practice of keeping a log.

- Earmark some space in your daily recovery journal or art journal, or simply set aside some pieces of paper for this process.

- This practice is generally done best at the end of each day when you can look back and reflect on what worked and what didn't work.

- You can keep a list with bullet points like this about the specific tasks you engaged in on any given day that seemed to help with your recovery. If you went to meetings as part of your day, note which meeting you attended, what you got out of it, and whether or not that meeting felt like a good fit.

- You can also note on the list what didn't feel especially helpful to your recovery on any given day (e.g., talking to a certain negative person, turning to a behavior for comfort that made you feel worse afterward).

- Some people like to approach this daily inventory with columns. If using this method, try to stay away from overtly judgmental language like "Good for Recovery" and "Bad for Recovery." Consider titling columns "Helpful"/"Unhelpful," "Healthy"/"Unhealthy," "Nourishing"/"Depleting," or any language that feels like the most helpful fit for you. To get away from the binary, you can even incorporate a middle third column that indicates which actions or behaviors may have been neutral or perhaps a little bit of both (e.g., attendance at a certain meeting, talking to a family member).

◆ Make a commitment to engage in this inventory for as long as feels appropriate, although a week is generally the minimum recommended timeframe. If you miss a day, please don't beat yourself up. You can always go back to it the next day.

Take a look at how Step Ten is worded and notice where some problems may exist for you. As in Step Four, the idea of inventory may prove problematic so consider replacing it with the idea of self-evaluation, or what yogis call self-study. If you've come this far in working the steps, we hope you realize by now that you can be kind to yourself, even when taking a look at your difficult stuff. The Tenth Step affirms that although we are not going to be perfect going forward, daily evaluation is imperative. Might framing it this way take some of the edge off about being wrong?

Admitting wrongdoing (the challenge of Step Ten) can prove difficult for those easily triggered by traumatic stimuli. Defensiveness can run high. One of the best places for an individual in early recovery to practice Step Ten is on the job. I remember in my early recovery, I found it so hard to admit when I was wrong at work because I took every bit of feedback, or every legitimate critique of my performance, as a personal insult. The more I addressed my trauma issues, the less and less I became triggered upon being criticized. I was thus better able to work Step Ten on a daily basis.[*]

How might this step be calling me to continue practicing discernment in recognizing where defensiveness is a block? What keeps me from admitting where I may be wrong today?

---

[*] Jamie Marich, *Trauma and the 12 Steps: An Inclusive Guide to Enhancing Recovery*, 86–87.

If this is your first time working Step Ten, what is prompting you to take this journey to the next level *now*? If you've worked this step before, what is your focus in this pass through the steps? What is the intention you are setting for how you would like your life to be different by working this step?

EXPRESSIVE ARTS OPTION: If freewriting alone on Step Ten does not feel sufficient, is there a way you can bring in another expressive practice (e.g., visual art, fiction or poetry writing, playlist construction, songwriting, dancing, or acting out a dramatic scene—even if it's something as simple as making a gesture or series of gestures that reflects what this step means to you at this point in your journey)? As a reminder, you may use a separate journal or other media for this process.

Using freewriting or an expressive arts practice of your choice, reflect on what gratitude you may be noticing for Step Ten and any thoughts, feelings, or sensations about your readiness to move to Step Eleven. Is there anything you may need to further prepare yourself for going on to the next step? Feel free to consult your "Step Zero" self-care inventory as a reference.

Step 11

Sought through prayer and meditation to improve our conscious contact with God as we understood Him,* praying only for knowledge of His† will for us and the power to carry that out.

What I love the most about Step Eleven is how it validates the practice of meditation as a lifeline of continued recovery. If I didn't learn all the different ways to meditate, I don't know if I would have stuck around twelve-step programs, especially when I struggled with the prayer part.

—Jamie

Having found Zen meditation in early recovery, I am someone who responds well to incense, candles, and other spiritual rituals. When not within reach of my spiritual objects at home, I seek to remind myself of my spiritual life any way I can. Whether it's carrying a book of Thomas Merton in my computer bag, whether it's a quick burst of mindfulness meditation at my desk, whether it's raising my gaze to the clouds—anything that provides me with a moment or more of prayer or meditation can change my perspective, sometimes profoundly. It has been more than worthwhile to make it a habit.

—Steve

---

* As a reminder, you can amend this language in any way you see fit.

† As a reminder, you can amend this language in any way you see fit.

MEDITATION: BODYFULNESS AND MOVEMENT

In this trauma-informed step workbook we've incorporated many meditations from the tradition of mindfulness—the art and practice of coming back to the present moment, without judgment. For many of us who practice yoga, dance, or other somatic healing methods, the concept of bodyfulness is just as vital. While drawing from the wisdom of mindfulness, *bodyfulness* (a term coined by Dr. Christine Caldwell) reminds us that coming home to our bodies is of utmost importance. The things we often do to cope with the legacy of unhealed trauma can cut us off from the essential information our bodies provide and what it can teach us about our experiences and ourselves. For many of us, being told unkind things about our body further increases this disconnect.

Learning to befriend your body and listen to its signals and wisdom can be a process in recovery. As you work on cultivating deeper levels of meditation in the Eleventh Step, we are encouraging you to really bring your body and its natural inclination to move into this process of connection. Even if you balked or got a little bit scared reading that last sentence, take pause and notice where you may have felt the "ping" in your body that registered scared or hesitant. That is what we mean by learning to listen to your body's signals. Your body will tell you what is going on with you well before your rational mind can compute what's going on.

This meditation utilizes a popular *T'ai Chi* form called *Painting Light*. Follow these steps to the level of your comfort, knowing that you are in control of how long you practice this at any one time. The practice can be done sitting, standing, or lying down. If you are immobile for any reason, you can rely on the power of your visual imagination to see and track the experience of light moving up and down your body and notice wherever any flickers of sensation may show up (e.g., in the eyes, on your face).

- In whatever position you choose (standing, sitting, or lying down), take a few moments to really rest into that position. Breathe. Notice the connection of your body to the surface on which you are standing, sitting, or lying down.

- On an inhale, draw both arms out in front of you about shoulder height. On the next natural inhale, draw the arms overhead as much as possible.

- On the next natural exhale, draw the hands and arms down, synchronized with the breath. Bring them down at least to the waist although you can go as low as the knees.

- On the next natural inhale, draw the hands and arms back up overhead, connected with breath.

- Continue with this natural movement for as long as you intend, bringing to mind the phrase *Painting Light*. Are there any colors you wish to visualize along with your movements?

- As a variation, you can add music and/or let the arms flow freely out to the sides or in different directions, coming back to the *Painting Light* form as you wrap up.

- Take at least thirty seconds, preferably longer, to stand (or sit) in silence and notice what you notice in the stillness after engaging in the movement. This noticing is the essence of meditation.

Take a look at how Step Eleven is worded and notice where some problems may exist for you. We certainly hope that some of the guided meditations in this book have helped you move through any barriers to meditating. However, for many people beginning their step work, the concept of *meditation* feels inaccessible. For others, being told specifically how to pray in this step is a major problem (while for countless others it's a comfort). Where do you stand on Step Eleven?

Step Eleven issues what is perhaps the greatest spiritual challenge of twelve-step recovery: "praying only for knowledge of God's will and the power to carry it out." Many of the struggles trauma survivors face in this step tend to be spiritual in nature. Some people battle with the spiritual aspects of recovery for quite some time, so they may still encounter the same challenges presented by Steps Two and Three with letting go of their self-sufficiency. Another problem for trauma survivors can show up in this step: the intricacy of God's will. Many trauma survivors have trouble with the concept of God's will because it may be nearly impossible to wrap their understanding around the notion that the traumatic experiences they endured were somehow God's will.†*

How has working the steps thus far impacted your feelings as you approach Step Eleven? If prayer and *Higher Power* don't work for you, has learning the various ways to meditate throughout this workbook helped to make a difference? If so, how?

---

* Alcoholics Anonymous World Services, *Alcoholics Anonymous*, 32.

† Jamie Marich, *Trauma and the 12 Steps: An Inclusive Guide to Enhancing Recovery*, 87.

If this is your first time working Step Eleven, what is prompting you to take this journey to the next level *now*? If you've worked this step before, what is your focus in this pass through the steps? What is the intention you are setting for how you would like your life to be different by working this step?

EXPRESSIVE ARTS OPTION: If freewriting alone on Step Eleven does not feel sufficient, is there a way you can bring in another expressive practice (e.g., visual art, fiction, or poetry writing, playlist construction, songwriting, dancing, or acting out a dramatic scene—even if it's something as simple as making a gesture or series of gestures that reflects what this step means to you at this point in your journey)? As a reminder, you may use a separate journal or other media for this process.

Using freewriting or an expressive arts practice of your choice, reflect on what gratitude you may be noticing for Step Eleven and any thoughts, feelings, or sensations about your readiness to move to Step Twelve. Is there anything you may need to further prepare yourself for going on to the next step? Feel free to consult your "Step Zero" self-care inventory as a reference.

Step 12

_____

Having had a spiritual awakening as the result of these steps, we tried to carry this message to alcoholic/addicted people* and to practice these principles in all our affairs.

Whether or not one likes the language of spiritual awakening (or doubts whether or not they've even had one), Step Twelve is about paying it forward. Sharing what you have received, and in that process, helping yourself over and over again. Although I've never been able to find an attribution, I once heard that you remember 5 percent of what you learn and 95 percent of what you teach. This plays out in every area of my life and sharing the program with others is no exception. Every time I share a part of my experience, strength, and hope with this path or help someone to work a step, I am hearing or reviewing exactly what I need to hear or to review at that given moment.

—Jamie

Even though I have had some very deep and moving encounters that I would call spiritual experiences, I most identify with the William James proposal of the educational variety. Each time I sit in a meeting with others who would otherwise remain in the trauma cycle, and we respectfully listen to each other and help one another, I feel like just this act defines spiritual experience quite completely. The other definition that I work with concerns boundaries. Trauma healing in the first eleven steps allows for being true to myself. And being true to myself is expressed through helping myself with my own oxygen mask before helping others in the cabin. Now I can be in the dance of life, the dance of recovery, the dance of ongoing healing and health.

—Steve

_____

* As a reminder, you can use whatever language works for you in this step.

Share Your Practice

If you have made it to this point in the book, you have now learned eleven different meditation strategies that you can use to prepare for each step. In the spirit of paying it forward that defines the Twelfth Step, we encourage you to take any one of the practices covered in this workbook and share it with someone in your circle—a sponsee, a friend, a client, or just someone you know in recovery. If your immediate reaction upon reading that directive is, "I can't teach meditation," take a breath into that reaction and then release it. To be clear, we are asking you to share the practice; share how you have received it in words that work for you (although you are more than welcome to read from this workbook as a guide).

Doing good Twelfth Step work is not about being perfect, it is about sharing—from the heart and from the depths of your experience, strength, and hope—what has worked for you. Be open to having the conversation with the person receiving what you share as to how they may need to modify different practices to work for them. This particular exercise is simply a training ground for the art of sharing that defines Step Twelve.

What did you notice about sharing a practice with someone else? Feel free to work your response to that question into any of the questions that follow for this step.

Take a look at how Step Twelve is worded and notice where some problems may exist for you. For many, it's not so much the wording as much as it is doubt—have I really had any kind of awakening, let alone a spiritual one? How can I translate what I've learned through the steps into my life? Write out your doubts—go with them and see what is revealed that is helping you learn this step.

Yes, a big part of Step Twelve is to carry the message to others who suffer. This does not mean that you become solely responsible for another's life or recovery. The step is not an open invitation for you to forget working on yourself as a sacrifice to others. The purpose of the Twelfth Step has always been to keep the person working it sober. . . . I've seen many people in recovery get caught up in the trap of reaching out to others in service at the expense of their own recovery. This is a problem we don't talk about enough in recovery settings and we need to address it more fully. The culprit is likely (you guessed it) unhealed trauma. *

Where do you see that tendency play out in your life and how can that be a problem for you in working Step Twelve? What are the differences between sharing what you've learned to help build up your recovery program versus just giving away every part of yourself to others?

---

* Jamie Marich, *Trauma and the 12 Steps: An Inclusive Guide to Enhancing Recovery*, 88.

If this is your first time working Step Twelve, what is prompting you to take this journey to the next level *now*? If you've worked this step before, what is your focus in this pass through the steps? What is the intention you are setting for how you would like your life to be different by working this step?

EXPRESSIVE ARTS OPTION: If freewriting alone on Step Twelve does not feel sufficient, is there a way you can bring in another expressive practice (e.g., visual art, fiction or poetry writing, playlist construction, songwriting, dancing, or acting out a dramatic scene—even if it's something as simple as making a gesture or series of gestures that reflects what this step means to you at this point in your journey)? As a reminder, you may use a separate journal or other media for this process.

Using freewriting or an expressive arts practice of your choice, reflect on what gratitude you may be noticing for Step Twelve and any hesitancy you may have about working this step. Feel free to consult your "Step Zero" self-care inventory as a reference.

Recommended Resources

Organizations and Recommended Websites

AA Agnostica: www.aaagnostica.org

AA Beyond Belief: www.beyondbelief.website

ACEs Connection: www.acesconnectioninfo.org

ACEs Too High: www.acestoohigh.com

An Infinite Mind: Dissociation Resources and Community; the Healing Together Conference:
    www.aninfinitemind.com

UCLA LGBTQ Campus Resource Center: lgbtq.ucla.edu/services-and-resources

Compassionate Recovery: www.compassionaterecovery.us

Dan Griffin: The Man Rules Podcast and Other Resources: www.dangriffin.com

Dancing Mindfulness: www.dancingmindfulness.com

DID Research: www.did-research.org

Gender Spectrum (Free Online Resources): www.genderspectrum.org

HealingTREE: Trauma Resources, Education & Empowerment: www.healingtreenonprofit.org

In The Rooms: Online Recovery Meetings and Support: www.intherooms.com

LifeRing Secular Recovery: www.lifering.org

Liv's Recovery Kitchen: www.livsrecoverykitchen.com

Medication-Assisted Recovery Anonymous: www.mara-international.org

NALGAP: The Association of Lesbian, Gay, Bisexual, Transgender Addiction Professionals and
    Their Allies: www.nalgap.org

Recovery 2.0: Life Beyond Addiction: www.r20.com

Recovery Dharma: www.recoverydharma.org

Refuge Recovery: www.refugerecovery.org

Secular AA: www.aasecular.org

Seeking Integrity (Dr. Rob Weiss): www.seekingintegrity.com/

Seeking Safety Model: www.treatment-innovations.org/seeking-safety.html

She Recovers: Self-Identified Women in Recovery: www.sherecovers.org

SMART Recovery: www.smartrecovery.org

SOS Sobriety: www.sossobriety.org

The Breathe Network: Healing Sexual Trauma: www.thebreathenetwork.org

The Plural Association/The Plural Warmline: www.pluralwarmline.org

The Trevor Project: www.thetrevorproject.org

Trauma and Dissociative Disorders Explained: www.traumadissociation.com

Trauma Made Simple/Trauma & the 12 Steps: The Official Resources Site of Dr. Jamie Marich: www.traumamadesimple.com

Trauma and the 12 Steps: Online Facebook Community: www.facebook.com/groups/2259777060801012

Wellbriety Movement: www.wellbriety.com

Women for Sobriety: www.womenforsobriety.org

Yoga of Recovery: www.yogaofrecovery.com

Yoga of Twelve Step Recovery (Y12SR): www.y12sr.com

Afterword

Flexible structure is exactly what the twelve steps offer—provided that a person is not rigidly interpreting the steps. Flexible structure is what an addicted survivor of trauma may need, in order to obtain solid footing on the road to recovery.

—JAMIE MARICH, *TRAUMA AND THE 12 STEPS: AN INCLUSIVE GUIDE TO ENHANCING RECOVERY*

What are you noticing now that you have worked through the steps using this format?

That question may open up a whole new stream of writing or inventory that you can journal on or use the expressive arts to explore! That is the beauty of working a recovery program whether or not the steps are specifically guiding you. There is always something more to explore. Living a lifestyle where you are committed to recovery is never about reaching a finish line. Rather, we can recognize that with each new season of challenges life may bring our way, we can rise to meet those challenges from a place of continued health and growth, or from old, reactionary patterns that kept us stuck for so long.

In our experience, working the steps is not a "one and done" exercise. You don't work them and then suddenly you get a medal, or a guarantee that your life in recovery will be marvelous forever. Hopefully by working the steps in the manner laid out in this workbook, you've been able to see that how you work a step at one point in your life may be different from how you are working it at another. And there is always room to grow and continue the work on yourself. For some people, this continued work in long-term recovery includes a yearly working through of the steps. For others, it's learning to listen to the subtle signals that say, "Something is amiss, I'd better take action," or "It's time to get back to basics," prompting a reworking of the steps.

We've prepared this workbook as a resource that can be used and adapted wherever you are in your journey. No matter how many times you work through it, we hope you discover something new and fresh on each pass through. Please remember that *Trauma and the 12 Steps: Daily Meditations and Reflections*[*] is another resource you can check out that can better help you work the steps in a day-to-day format. As we teach throughout our work, a small amount of practice on a consistent, daily basis is much better for us overall than doing nothing for days or weeks on end and then spending a big chunk of time on meditation or another recovery endeavor.

We hope you find this wisdom to be a useful inspiration for the road ahead.

---

[*] Jamie Marich and Stephen Dansiger, *Trauma and the 12 Steps: Daily Meditations and Reflections* (Warren, OH: Creative Mindfulness Media, 2020).

About the Authors

Dr. Jamie Marich (she/they) is a woman in long-term recovery from an addictive disorder and is living loudly and proudly as a woman with a dissociative disorder with the goal of smashing discrimination about dissociation in the mental health field and in society at large. Jamie began her career as a humanitarian aid worker in Bosnia and Herzegovina from 2000–2003, primarily teaching English and music. She travels internationally teaching on topics related to trauma, EMDR therapy, expressive arts, mindfulness, and yoga, while maintaining a private practice and online education operations in her home base of northeast Ohio. Jamie is the founder of the Institute for Creative Mindfulness and the developer of the Dancing Mindfulness approach to expressive arts therapy. She is the developer of Yoga for Clinicians.

Jamie is the author of *EMDR Made Simple: 4 Approaches to Using EMDR with Every Client* (2011); *Trauma and the Twelve Steps: A Complete Guide to Enhancing Recovery* (2012); *Creative Mindfulness: 20+ Strategies for Wellness & Recovery* (2013); *Trauma Made Simple: Competencies in Assessment, Treatment and Working with Survivors* (2014); *Dancing Mindfulness: A Creative Path to Healing and Transformation* (2015); and *Process Not Perfection: Expressive Arts Solutions for Trauma Recovery* (2019). She coauthored *EMDR Therapy and Mindfulness for Trauma-Focused Care* with colleague Dr. Stephen Dansiger in 2018; as well as *Trauma and the 12 Steps: Daily Meditations and Reflections* (2020); and *Healing Addiction with EMDR Therapy: A Trauma-Focused Guide* (2021). North Atlantic Books published a revised and expanded edition of *Trauma and the 12 Steps: An Inclusive Guide to Enhancing Recovery* in summer 2020; and also published *Transforming Trauma with Jiu-Jitsu: A Guide for Survivors, Therapists, and Jiu-Jitsu Practitioners to Facilitate Embodied Recovery* (with Anna Pirkl, 2022); and *Dissociation Made Simple: A Stigma-Free Guide to Embracing Your Dissociative Mind and Navigating Daily Life* (2023).

The *New York Times* featured Jamie's writing and work on *Dancing Mindfulness* in 2017 and 2020. NALGAP: The Association of Lesbian, Gay, Bisexual, Transgender Addiction Professionals and Their Allies awarded Jamie with their esteemed President's Award in 2015 for her work as an LGBT advocate. The EMDR International Association (EMDRIA) granted Jamie the 2019 Advocacy in EMDR Award for her use of her public platform in the media and in the addiction field to advance awareness about EMDR therapy and to reduce stigma around mental health.

Photo by Gen Max

Dr. Stephen Dansiger (he/him) is a rocker who got sober in the late 1980s and then became a sought-after clinician, writer, and meditation teacher. He is the creator and founder of the MET(T)A Protocol (Mindfulness and EMDR Treatment Template for Agencies), which utilizes the frameworks of Buddhist psychology, mindfulness, and EMDR therapy to create an agency's primary clinical practice system. After fifteen years as a Diversity Equity Inclusion and Justice trainer, He became an EMDRIA Approved Consultant and Certified Therapist, providing EMDR Training and Advanced Topic workshops as Senior Faculty for the Institute for Creative Mindfulness. Stephen is the author of *Clinical Dharma: A Path for Healers and Helpers* (2016), *EMDR Therapy and Mindfulness for Trauma-Focused Care* (coauthored with Jamie Marich) (2018), and *Mindfulness for Anger Management: Transformative Skills for Overcoming Anger and Managing Powerful Emotions* (2018); in addition to coauthoring with Jamie *Trauma and the 12 Steps: Daily Meditations and Reflections* (2020) and *Healing Addiction with EMDR Therapy: A Trauma-Focused Guide* (2021). He avidly blogs and podcasts on topics related to mental health, recovery, and mindfulness. In addition to maintaining a private practice in Los Angeles, Stephen travels internationally, speaking and teaching on Buddhist mindfulness, EMDR therapy, the MET(T)A Protocol, trauma, and clinician self-care. He has been practicing Buddhist mindfulness for almost thirty years, and teaches dharma classes regularly in Los Angeles and at other centers internationally. Stephen is also innovating in digital health technology for mental health and beyond, having earned a masters in health care innovation from the University of Pennsylvania.

About North Atlantic Books

North Atlantic Books (NAB) is an independent, nonprofit publisher committed to a bold exploration of the relationships between mind, body, spirit, and nature. Founded in 1974, NAB aims to nurture a holistic view of the arts, sciences, humanities, and healing. To make a donation or to learn more about our books, authors, events, and newsletter, please visit www.northatlanticbooks.com.